# Pinned!

## Farm Accident—Our Walk in Faith

GEORGE AND KAYE TOPP

WestBow Press books may be ordered through booksellers or by contacting:

WestBow Press
A Division of Thomas Nelson & Zondervan
1663 Liberty Drive
Bloomington, IN 47403
www.westbowpress.com
1 (866) 928-1240

Because of the dynamic nature of the Internet, any web addresses or links contained in this book may have changed since publication and may no longer be valid. The views expressed in this work are solely those of the author and do not necessarily reflect the views of the publisher, and the publisher hereby disclaims any responsibility for them.

Scripture quotations taken from The Holy Bible, New International Version® NIV® Copyright © 1973 1978 1984 2011 by Biblica, Inc. TM. Used by permission. All rights reserved worldwide.

The Authorized (King James) Version of the Bible ('the KJV'), the rights in which are vested in the Crown in the United Kingdom, is reproduced here by permission of the Crown's patentee, Cambridge University Press. The Cambridge KJV text including paragraphing, is reproduced here by permission of Cambridge University Press.

ISBN: 978-1-9736-8048-2 (sc)
ISBN: 978-1-9736-8818-1 (e)

Library of Congress Control Number: 2020904765

Printed in the United States of America.

WestBow Press rev. date: 07/07/2020

WESTBOW
P R E S S®
A DIVISION OF THOMAS NELSON
& ZONDERVAN

Over the course of my 36 year career in Rehabilitation Medicine I have cared for many hundreds of trauma victims. George's injury was however a very unique one. I'm not sure that his event could be replicated if you tried. This memoir chronicles a journey that is a testament to the strength of the human spirit when supported by faith, family, and friends. His recovery course was quite remarkable and in no small part related to his "can do" attitude reinforced by his faith, that continued to grow throughout the process. The road to recovery was not always smooth and George experienced some of the emotional healing that often needs to occur with the physical healing in these events. As I often related to many of our patients "We will make the most of what we have today and hope for a better tomorrow". George clearly did just that. With his life partner Kaye by his side and strength from above he made the most of every tomorrow. My wife has a plaque on a desk in our home that I look at each morning, it states, "Faith makes all things possible". That was clearly the case for George.

William N Klava M.D.

To our grandchildren, Ryan, Kyle, Justin, Ethan, Paige, Garrett, Cora, Calli, Cailyn, Jaden, Gavin, and Tegan, Whom we love so dearly. And to my wife, I love you, I love you, I love you. I haven't said it nearly enough. And to our son, Corey, and his wife, Rhonda; our daughters, Andrea, Karen, and Elizabeth (Liz), and their husbands, Marlen, Tad, and Craig. You are all such a blessing to us.

# Contents

George wrote his story in January 2005 and shared it when giving his testimony to a number of groups. Transcriptions are from his audio journal, taped while he was in rehabilitation in June 2004. CaringBridge entries were written by Elizabeth, daughter, and Kaye. Kaye's entries, doctor reports and consultations, and medical information were taken from Kaye's journal.

# Acknowledgments

Thank you to the doctors, nurses, and support staff at the Carrington Hospital and MeritCare for the excellent care given to me. Thank you, Liz, for writing accounts in CaringBridge. I was thankful for all the prayers and messages. There were more than eight thousand hits on the website during my hospital stay, and we continued to use it until the end of the summer. Thank you to Bev and Dave for giving Kaye the comfort of your home, and to Dave for your expert doctor's advice in delaying surgery to close my wounds. The discussions that took place resulted in a change of course and no skin grafts. To Muriel, who one day at the hospital said, "What a story. You should write a book." To a special nurse, Julie, who touched my heart with her story, and I touched her heart with mine. Thank you, Julie, for the inspirational painting. Thank you to our pastors and our neighbors and friends (our good community), who farmed, ranched, and did so many other things to help us while we were both away from the farm and during my recovery at home.

Kaye worked as a Title 1 teacher at Midkota Public School. We were grateful that Kerwin Borgen, superintendent, and Jeanne Hoyt, elementary principal, allowed Kaye to remain with George until the end of the school year and so appreciated Glenda Hoeckle, kindergarten and Title 1 teacher, who completed Title 1 year-end work. In grades seven through twelve, the kids often asked how George was doing. "When it was a good report, they would show thumbs-up as they went down the hall," said Diane Lyman, the Midkota office manager.

Thank you to family and friends who helped edit our book and to all who have supported our efforts with love and prayers. The desire of our hearts is to bring glory to God and to know that He is pleased. We believe David's words in Psalm 62:11–12a (NIV), "One thing God has spoken, two things I have heard: 'Power belongs to you, God, and with you, Lord, is unfailing love.'"

# Introduction: The Independent Farmer

My father, grandfather, and great-grandfather were farmers, so you might say I was born into it. I could work in the great outdoors and watch nature all around me. I was my own boss and didn't have to punch a clock. As a farmer, I could be envied because I was seen as living a more tranquil life and appeared to be more carefree because I had very few people to answer to other than myself.

This rugged individualism was good, but it was also harmful when I allowed pride and lack of humility to affect my relationship with other people, and more importantly with God. At times, I could easily think, *I don't need God or anyone else. I can do it myself.*

This is a story about how God got my attention. It's about His goodness, mercy, and healing during and following my near-fatal accident. Jeremiah 29:13 (NIV) says, "You will seek me and find me when you seek me with all your heart." I sought Him with all of my being, and He reached out His hand and rescued me.

# The Truck

The headline of the March 2005 issue of *Dakota Farmer* says, "Six die on DK [Dakota] farms in 2004."

MERIBETH BALSDON holds a picture of her late husband, who made everything fun," says Meribeth of her husband, who dryer. He had suffocated and suffered a heart attack.

Well, I could have been number seven, except for the grace of God. My accident happened on May 3, 2004, at our farm near Grace City, North Dakota. It started out as a typical spring day. I had about a half dozen cows left to calf, and I was busy finishing up seeding barley. My wife, Kaye, and I were small grain farmers and raised beef cattle in the east central part of the state. We grew wheat, barley, and oats and had a herd of stock cows, which calved out in the spring. We pastured the cows and calves in the warm months, fed them hay and oats in the winter, and sold the calves in January.

Right from the start, I'm going to tell you I'm half-German and half-Norwegian and a very independent farmer. In other words, I depended on myself to get things done. It wasn't always that way. I grew up farming with my dad, Ervin, and then took over the farm from Dad as a young adult. Dad continued to work with me until his death, when I was forty years old. Our son, Corey, farmed with me until he graduated from college and moved to Minneapolis. Kaye and our daughters helped when they could, but gradually, I had more work to do than I had time.

As my own boss, I answered to no one. I didn't have to ask anyone else things like, "Will this work or do you think this …?" I was willingly to take advice from others but was in the habit of going ahead on my own and getting the job done as best I could without stopping to ask for help. Many times, we farmers have the attitude of "I can do it myself." I was about to find out how that way of thinking would get me into very serious trouble.

On that first Monday morning in early May, I checked the cows that were calving and was heading out of the farmyard to seed barley in a field near Lester Wright's old farm, which is about a mile north of the farm. I had been having some problems starting our 1967 International two-ton, single-axle truck. The truck was used to transfer seed and fertilizer to the grain drill (seeder) in the field. It was new when Dad (Ervin) bought it, but after many years of use, like all machinery, it had parts that were wearing out. I had removed the truck box and put the drill fill on back because the flatbed was the right size to hold the two hoppers. The drill fill, fertilizer, and grain added about four tons of weight to the truck.

I managed to get the truck going, drove out to the field, filled the seeder, and began planting barley. About noon, I jumped in the truck, sat down into the seat's hole that extended to the springs below, turned the key, and drove the old International back home. I parked it near the house and walked into the house to eat lunch.

In foreground: International 666.
In background: 1967 International single-axle truck with drill fill (two hoppers).

After I had eaten and was ready to go back out to the field, I went out to start the truck, but don't you know, it wouldn't start. I grabbed the jumper cables and attached them to the battery posts and tried again. It still didn't start.

So here is where my independence got me into trouble. I got the bright idea that I could pull the truck with my small loader tractor (International 666—no cab) and a chain to get it started. That idea was good enough in itself, but doing this by oneself and not having someone drive the truck is a dumb (independent farmer) idea.

I stood on the tractor's platform, which is near to the ground and to the left of the tractor's steering wheel. If the truck started, I had the intention of jumping off the platform, running back to the truck, and taking the truck out of gear. Well, my second mistake was using too short of a chain. Now, how many mistakes does one person get? Let me tell you, this was the first time that I tried that and, needless to say, my last time.

With my right arm stretched across the top of the steering wheel, I grasped the handle of the hydrostatic lever, which is a gear that operates with oil. I pushed the lever forward and slowly edged the tractor ahead. The truck started right up and caught up to the tractor. You can't believe how fast a truck can go in super low! The bumper hit the rear wheels of the tractor. I panicked right then and put the hydrostatic lever into neutral.

The truck, still pushing the tractor, climbed up the back wheels in an instant, crushing the steering wheel and the seat. While all this was happening within a blink of an eye, I dove forward, with my belly landing on the hood of the tractor. My knees were about six inches ahead of the steering wheel, and the upper part of my legs (midthigh) were on top of a three-inch pipe that acts as a brace for the loader.

The bumper of the truck landed right on top of the back of my legs and that three-inch pipe.

I was instantly pinned. The truck continued to push the tractor about fifteen feet, and then the motor died. I was able to reach down and turn the petcock valve off for the gas on the tractor, and in about one minute, the tractor shut off.

I was pinned between my knees to my hips. I saw no blood. There was intense stabbing, burning pain in my legs with very sharp pain at my knees. I began to shake. My legs started getting numb. I was still clearheaded but could only think of the pain.

The time was 1:00 p.m. My bag phone was in the truck.

The truck's front wheels traveled up the
tractor's back wheels and stopped.

The steering wheel and seat were crushed,
and one hydraulic lever was broken.

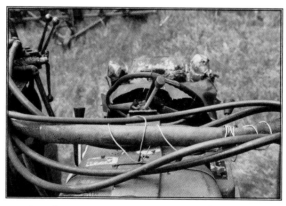

My legs lay across the bar (middle of the picture),
with my feet pointing toward the tractor seat. My
legs crossed the bar, six inches above my knees.

I was lying face down along the left side of the tractor hood.

Skid marks from the tractor.

We live on a seldom-used gravel road, so my hope for someone to drive by was slim to none. The Spickler Ranch was having their annual bull sale that day, so most of my neighbors were at the sale. Also, Kaye, who was a teacher, was in Fargo (140 miles away) for a meeting. I didn't expect her back until five or six o'clock that evening. I was wearing a light jacket. The temperature was in the midfifties. It was sunny off and on.

I kept a watch in the pocket of my bib overalls. I looked at the watch about every five minutes until three o'clock. Also in that pocket was my calving notepad, where I kept track of the calves that were born. I began writing my goodbyes to my wife and family in the tablet shortly after one o'clock.

To keep from going into shock, I grabbed the loader bars on each side of the tractor hood and lifted up. I did this repeatedly. I did it to counter the pain or divert my focus from the pain.

I did a lot of praying while I was pinned. I will tell you right now I had faith before that day, but Monday, May 3, 2004, turned out to be the day that I found out I was powerless. It was only through the grace of God that I survived.

This is what I wrote in the tablet during my time on the tractor. Because I was in constant pain, I was only able to write two or three words at a time.

Actual Size
3" x 5"

Actual size
4 1/4" x 1/4"

(Note the amount of lead at end of pencil.)

Kobe
I went to
start the
truck I
Love you
my legs

are pinned
it is about
1:90 pm
I hope
someone
comes

the truck
come up on
over the
cricks
I shut
the tracker
off

11

I pray
to God
My legs
heart so
they are

Going numb
this week
wont stop
and I pulled
it.

I love
each and
everyone of
you come
Rhonda
Ryran Kyle
Justin

Andrea
Marlou
paige
I pray to
God
I love

Karen
Tad
Lizt
Craig
Why didn't

I get out
of the way
I can't
pull my
self out

pleas God
send
some one
here
Starter
the Truck

isn't working
on my legs
hurt
I shut the
gas off on
the tractor

Jesus
Christ
pleasetake
love you
I took

the truth
out of
grace th
truth come
up over

nevertheless
so fast
I cant
get out
of the way

I pray for
eacht
every one
of you
of the pain

send someon
here
I love
you so
Roger

you have
so much
love to
give.
find someone
+ show it

I'm quaky
all the
time
I wish
I would
lose conciou

I shake
so much
don't know
what to
do

15

I might
end my
life with
a knife
or the
power

pain
I shake
so
please
God send
somedie

2:00pm
I want
help now
please help
me

Kayla is
intigo

I go in
and out

Ed
God for
give me
for my
sins
or the pain

I must
hold on
can't take
it

I'll see
you in
heaven
if only

I could
die
in & out
in & out

17

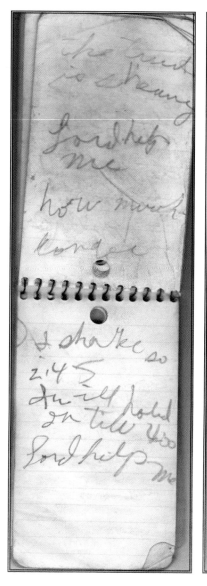

19

put pills
on by dismal
wind
I must
hold on on

I start
gas off on

broctan
3:05
@ the pain
in my right
leg

kids be so
good to your
family love
your wives
sweethearts
I love you
all

Lord give
me strength
to hang on
to die is
the coward
way out

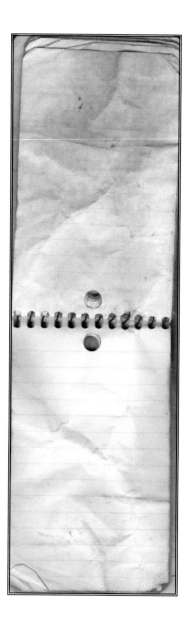

Here are my notes transcribed:

> Kaye, I went to start the truck. I love you. My legs are pinned. It is about 1:00 p.m. I hope someone comes. The truck came up over the wheels. I shut the tractor off. I pray to God. My legs hurt so. They are going numb. The truck won't start, so I pulled it. I love each and every one of you. Corey, Rhonda, Ryan, Kyle, Justin, Andrea, Marlen, Paige. I pray to God. I love Karen and Tad, Liz and Craig.
>
> Why didn't I get out of the way? I can't pull myself out. Please God send someone here. Starter on truck isn't working. Oh, my legs hurt. I shut the gas off on the tractor. Jesus Christ please take care of me. I took the tractor out of gear; the truck came up over the wheels so fast. I couldn't get out of the way. I pray for each and every one of you. Oh, the pain. Send someone here. I love you so, Kaye. You have so much love to give, find someone and share it. I'm awake all the time. I wish I would lose consciousness. I shake so much. Don't know what to do. I might end my life with a knife. Oh, the pain. I shake so. Please God send someone. 2:00 p.m. I must hold on. Please help me. Kaye is in Fargo. I go in and out. God forgive me for my sins. Oh the pain. I must hold on. Can't take it. I'll see you in Heaven. If only I could die.
>
> In and out … In and out … Oh the pain. Kaye, share your life with someone. Love you so. 2:20 p.m. Time goes so slow. Nobody comes by. I wish the pain would stop. 2:30 Love you so. The truck is heavy. Lord help me. How much longer? I shake so. 2:45 I will hold on till 4:00. Lord help me. If I can stand the

pain. I won't bleed to death. I will make it. So thirsty. Oh man send someone. [Here are some instructions that I wrote for Kaye:] Fix starter on the truck. Put belts on bi-directional. I must hold on. I shut gas off on tractor. 3:05 Oh the pain in my right leg. Kids, be so good to your family. Love your wife and husbands. I love you all. Lord give me strength to hang on. To die is a coward's way out. Don't know if I can make it. I pray for our church bless. Oh my, please help me. 3:25 God please send someone soon.

I was focusing my attention on my watch for the first two and a half hours because I looked at my watch every five minutes. At about two thirty, I hit a low point. I had a knife. I just about ended my life. At that low point, I came to the realization that to take my life would be a coward's way out. I would never do that to my family.

Then, at three thirty, I dropped my pencil. I felt completely lost, desolate, and alone. I lost contact with my family and the world, but I didn't lose contact with God.

I had a strong feeling that God would never give me more pain than I could bear. I felt as long as there was pain, I still might be getting some circulation to my toes. I looked at my legs and said to God, "They aren't broken. I'm not bleeding to death." It was at that point I turned everything over to God. I said, "God, You are not through with me yet. I will make it. Come what may." Then I said, "Thy will be done."

You cannot believe the total peace that came over me. There was no pain.

I didn't look at my watch until five o'clock. What occurred between three thirty and five is somewhat of a mystery to me. I believe that Jesus overrode the pain during that time, but at five o'clock, I had pain again. I took my knife out of its sheath and scratched "500" on the hood of the tractor. I scratched the time because I didn't know if I would be alive when Kaye got home. I put the knife back in the sheath and waited for Kaye.

"500" (5:00 p.m.) on the hood of the tractor.

Then, I eyed up the situation. Because of the constant pain, I had to get the truck off me. The front of the truck had come up over the tractor tires and down on me. With the truck tires lined up perfectly over the tractor tires, I knew when it was backed up, the truck had to lift back up over the tires. I figured when Kaye got there, I would have her back the truck off the tractor and me. I would have to be careful with Kaye because she was squeamish and had fainted at the sight of blood, but I had confidence that she could drive it off.

It was from five o'clock on that I really struggled to keep from going into shock. My skin was cold and clammy, and uncontrollable shaking gripped me. I felt waves of radiating pain from my knees to my toes. During this whole ordeal, I wasn't scared. I kept telling myself, "Just keep hanging on, just keep hanging on."

Kaye drove into the yard at about six o'clock. She stopped the car in the driveway and came running. I heard her say my name. I talked to her in very calm words. "Get into the truck. See if it starts. I don't know if it will start, but if it does, you put it in reverse—you know where the reverse is—and you back it off and don't stop until it hits the ground." She said no, she'd go and get our neighbor, Dennis, who lived a half mile away. I repeated my words to her in the same manner. "No, you get into the truck. You start the truck and put it in reverse, and you don't stop until you hit the ground."

She got into the truck, although I don't know how she did it, as the running board was about five feet off the ground. It started right up even though the key had been turned on the entire five hours. (Thank you, God.) She put it in reverse. There was extreme pain in my legs as the truck bumper retreated. I don't know how I kept from being pulled off the tractor.

Then the bumper lifted as the truck wheels rolled up over the tractor wheels and bounced on the ground. I clung to that three-inch pipe with my arms and belly. My legs hung down by the axle and felt like a couple of tree stumps and not part of my body. I asked Kaye for a glass of water because I was so thirsty. I was relieved to be free but was still in pain. I knew everything was not going to be okay. Kaye left to get Dennis.

I've known Dennis for many years. Before moving to the farm half a mile east of us, Dennis worked as a hired man on my cousin's farm and ranch operation at Grace City. Dennis is a hardworking and very helpful neighbor. He's Johnny-on-the spot and doesn't question your directions but follows them.

He came up to me and asked me if we should call an ambulance. I told him, "No. Get my legs off this axle." They looked like a couple of tree stumps to me. They felt twice as big as normal. "Help me down off this tractor and drag me into the car. I'm not waiting twenty-five minutes for an ambulance." Dennis helped Kaye get me off the tractor, and he dragged me to the car while Kaye climbed in the back seat and pulled me in.

As Dennis drove into Carrington, he kept asking me, "Are you okay, George?" I was shivering and incoherent most of the time. My legs were totally numb from my knees down to my toes. (I can still feel that sensation whenever I think about that, even years after the accident.) I heard Dennis and Kaye talking and knew Dennis was driving very fast. I could feel the speed but didn't notice the curves or bumps on the road. It didn't seem long until we got to the hospital.

We arrived at the emergency room at six thirty. Four personnel lifted me onto a backboard and then a cot and rolled me into the ER. The nurses pulled off my boots and cut my pant legs as one of them reported, "You aren't going to use these pants again." My blood pressure was 138/65 and pulse rate was 106/minute. I was visibly shaking. I answered their questions and described the incident, denying loss of consciousness during the five hours on the tractor. The level of my pain was at a 10 on a 1–10 scale. I was given morphine. The x-rays showed no fractures. Dr. James Craig, attending physician, Carrington Health Center Emergency Room Note Assessment: "Significant crush injury at the mid thigh to both lower extremities with hypesthesia and inability to move the legs from that area on distally." Dr. Craig called for a Life Flight helicopter.

I got a chopper ride to Fargo. I don't remember anything about the trip except that it was noisy with the constant whump-whump-whump of the helicopter blades. The helicopter landed on the roof of MeritCare hospital, and I was taken into the preoperative holding area. There I was diagnosed with bilateral compartment syndrome of the bilateral thigh and calf, secondary to crush injury. I had developed rhabdomyolysis and acute renal failure and was in critical condition. Elizabeth, our daughter, and her husband, Craig, were with me. The staff was busy getting me ready for emergency surgery. Dr. Kubalak, general surgeon, told me if he needed to amputate my legs, it would happen during surgery. I talked to Glenda, my sister, and Kaye on the phone and was hurried into the operating room for surgery.

The standard treatment for an acute compartment syndrome (crush injury) is a fasciotomy. To do this, surgeons make long incisions in the fascia (thick layers of tissue) to release the pressure building inside. Muscles are in bags, many bags in a larger bag. The larger bag (outside skin) has to be cut to relieve the pressure. The length of cuts on my legs totaled seven feet, four inches. (See Kaye's journal, appendix 1.)

When I awoke the next morning in ICU, the nurse told me she was surprised how well I did during the hours following surgery. I had a good night's sleep. A tube had been inserted, so I couldn't drink any water, but I wasn't in much pain and could move my hands when instructed and make myself comfortable. Although I was able to move my legs for the doctor, amputation was still in the picture. I would be monitored closely for the next twenty-four hours, as they wouldn't wait too long to set my prostheses. (See Kaye's journal, appendix 2.)

I was in ICU a total of five days, with a tube in my mouth and down my throat. I don't remember too much of the first two days, but I do remember a friend coming in on Wednesday. With the tube in my mouth, I couldn't talk, but I was given a piece of paper and pencil, and I wrote, "Pray for me."

It was about that time I came to the realization that God really had a plan for my life. I could relate back to the total peace that came over me on the tractor. God's peace gave me hope, faith, and determination. I also remembered the time when I was twenty-six years old. I had surgery to remove ganglion cysts on both of my wrists and was diagnosed with rheumatoid arthritis that was dormant (inactive). It was at this time that I asked Jesus to come into my life and, because of my mom's illness, prayed that I would never lose the use of my legs. My mom had rheumatoid arthritis and eventually could no longer walk. The remembrance of this prayer was magnified because of the accident. The prayer and the total peace that I felt gave me the faith and the will to believe that I would be completely healed. By the time I got out of ICU five days later, I had complete faith that I would recover fully.

Pastor Kevin Ryoo, from Edgewood United Methodist, Fargo, Darrell and Dee's (Kaye's parents) church, came in to see me. Later, Pastor Kevin read scripture with our family and friends. He talked about the courage Joshua had in crossing the river and prayed.

Our daughter Karen arrived from Arizona, and Kaye's sister, Bev, started a CaringBridge site for me. Both Elizabeth and Kaye wrote updates on the site.

I rested well the second night. The doctor was concerned about my muscle tissue and kidneys. Kaye, Andrea, Karen, Liz, and Bev came to see me at eight o'clock in the morning. As they all walked into the room, Kaye jokingly told my male nurse, "There *are* men in his life!" Later, Dave, my brother-in law and a dermatologist, pushed on my toes. Color came back fast, which was good because it meant there was capillary action. Corey, our son, arrived at noon with Kyle, our five-year-old grandson who wanted to come. (See Kaye's journal, appendix 3.)

> CaringBridge, Wednesday, May 5, 2004 2:53 PM CDT—At 2:00 p.m. Dr. Kubalak met with us. Dad's muscle tissue looks good. His right leg looks better than his left. His left calf muscle does have some brown tissue, but not significant enough to require amputation at this time. The body is able to absorb some dead muscle tissue by forming scar tissue within the body, and this is natural for the body to

do. Dr. Kubalak wants to wait a while to see how the muscle continues to heal, but it is doubtful how much function will return to his leg muscles. Dad will probably start weaning off the vent and decrease his sedation to be more alert. So this will help when the rehab doctor comes to test the nerves and muscle groups which will give them an idea of how much function may return. Dr. Kubalak believes that it would be better for Dad to have function through prosthetic legs rather than having healthy muscle tissue in his legs with no function. This is a major decision that is not easy to make. When Dad comes out of sedation, he will be able to think about this. We are thankful that we don't have to decide. We all believe that no matter what happens, Dad has the will to make it through. He has made it this far, not on his own strength, but God's. And anything is possible with God.

As far as his kidneys go, his labs have been a little high, which show some damage to the kidneys. There may be need for some short term dialysis. This is kind of a wait-and-see situation as well.

A plastic surgeon also came to see Dad this afternoon about doing skin grafts to close the open wounds. Skin grafts would reduce the chance of infection and would speed up the healing process. They plan to start this on Monday, if all goes well.

Dad has been complaining of being thirsty. The nurses have been able to moisten his mouth every now and then. They have tied Dad's hands down because he tries to pull the breathing tube out. He is very anxious to get rid of it! The nurse asked Dad if he could trust him to not pull the tube out, and Dad shook his head "no" and laughed! It was pretty funny. So the restraints remain.

When I awoke on the third morning in ICU, I saw Kaye sitting next to my bed. I smiled at her with my eyes. Corey and Karen came in. The day before, I was so sedated that this was the first time I really saw Corey. These were special times with the kids and Kaye. They are a blessing! Kyle, Corey's five-year-old son, gave me a picture he had drawn and colored. Paige, Andrea's two-year-old daughter, was a little afraid of seeing me in bed hooked up to equipment. Corey explained that the drill fill added additional weight to the back end of the truck. The front end was elevated and contributed to the truck's wheels catching hold of the tractor wheels when it lunged forward.

The doctor changed my bandages. The tissue looked good. I had some muscle function in my thighs. This was more hopeful than two days ago. The nurse said the doctor was pretty excited when he saw that I could move my knees up a little. The tissue in my left calf hadn't gotten any worse. My kidney function had stabilized, though was still less than 50 percent. Elizabeth asked if I was at peace. She explained to me everything that had happened and what would happen medically.

My breathing tube was taken out on the fourth day in ICU. This meant I could finally drink water and talk. Nurse Joe said, "There wasn't a lot of bruising, and the tissue looked nice and pink." When there was a need for a skin graft, it would be taken from my back. It would cover an opening, still allowing for the swelling to go down, as well as preventing infection. Friends came from home. I told them I had excruciating pain and throbbing all the time. I didn't know how I kept from being pulled back when Kaye backed the truck off of me. Elizabeth and Kaye talked with me about taking antidepressants because of the trauma and physical therapy to follow. I never took them, but it was important to have the discussion. Corey talked to Jeff Topp, my cousin and friend, about the farming that needed to be done.

Rhonda, Justin, Kyle, and Ryan came up to the hospital. Ron Nelson, my brother-in-law, offered to take family members out to the farm at noon the next day for the community Work Day. Karen and Kaye were going to go, but on the advice of Dave, they decided to stay near me.

> CaringBridge, Friday, May 7, 2004 6:41 PM CDT—
> This morning Mom, Bev, and Corey were visiting with Dad and his male nurse. The nurse indicated to Dad that he should finally be able to eat solid food later today, but since Dad was so well fed through the tube, he wouldn't be that hungry. Dad rolled his eyes at him saying, "Yeah, right!!" Bev mentioned that maybe they would need to put the restraints back on his hands so that he didn't eat too much, too quickly. The nurse then said he was going to put the restraints back on his hands, not for eating food, but to make sure that Dad doesn't go after him! Dad was laughing the whole time.
>
> Today he is able to lift his legs off the bed a few inches. Dr. Kubalak noticed stronger muscle contractions than yesterday. Dad is still not able to move his calf muscles. He has been moving his legs quite a bit while he lies in bed.

Bev and Dave came to see me the following morning. It was the first opportunity for me to tell someone what happened. We talked, cried, and hugged. This was also the same day that friends and neighbors from our community came to our farm for a Work Day. At first it was difficult for me to give up control of seeding the crop, but after our son,

Corey, explained things to me, I soon realized that I needed to accept what they planned to do. The men seeded soybeans and worked cattle, giving shots to the calves and getting them ready for the pasture. The Schoolhouse Café provided the lunch, and the women helped serve it. Days earlier, Leon Wright, our neighbor, finished seeding barley, and during the upcoming summer months, neighbors sprayed my crops, put up the hay, and took care of the cattle. Our friends and neighbors were so good to us. They literally dropped their busy schedules and came to help with the seeding and with the cattle. They gave their time and resources in preparing for the day and making it happen. I was overwhelmed by their generosity. (See Kaye's journal, appendixes 4-5.)

CaringBridge, Saturday, May 8, 2004 6:59 PM CDT—Dad is keeping the nurses on their toes with his humor. He is very happy to be where he is at right now. Dad said he had enough "pull" to request Joe, his nurse from ICU, to transfer with him, even if Joe wasn't the prettiest one he's seen. He really has enjoyed giving Joe a hard time, but he also knows when to stop so that Joe won't refuse to give him water! Dad and our family are very overwhelmed with all of the support back home. We thank all of you, from the bottom of our hearts, who worked cattle and finished his seeding, fence fixing, lawn mowing, garage sweeping, raking, etc., etc., all in one day. This is a miracle. Thank you all who have been praying. As you can see, God is continually performing miracles for our dad and family. We give Him all the glory and praise for this. "Those who know your name trust in you; for you, LORD, have not forsaken those who seek you." Psalm 9:10 NIV

Farm Work Day.

Dennis Hofmann, Leon Wright, and Alan Scanson.

Working cattle.

Seeding soybeans.

Lunch served by Grace City Ladies and
Grace City Schoolhouse café.

Neighbors and friends.
International truck with drill fill (in background).

Just after getting out of ICU, Jessi Black, our daughter Karen's childhood classmate, came to see me. She would be getting married on October 16, 2004. Karen would be a bridesmaid. I looked Jessi right in the eye and told her, "I will be dancing at your wedding dance." I do like to dance, but those words had to be God inspired because there was no way for me to know.

Earlier, Corey had told me that the surgeon was very concerned the first few days about me losing my legs. I wasn't surprised by the news because before going into surgery, Dr. Kubalak said they would amputate my legs at that time if needed. A crush injury can cause muscle tissue to break down and creatinine levels in the blood to rise, which may result in kidney damage. The normal level for creatinine is 1, and 3 is critical. Mine was 2.9 and never rose any higher. A crush injury also damages the muscles so that they no longer function, which would be another reason to amputate. (See Kaye's journal, appendixes 6–7.)

# The Wounds

Next, those open wounds had to be sewn up. I was still in ICU when the plastic surgeon came in and told me about the procedure. I didn't remember much of what he said because of the morphine and sleeping pill. I had tubes in my mouth and couldn't talk. Kaye wasn't there to ask questions.

Surgery was scheduled for Monday, May 10, which was one week following my accident. Several days before surgery, Dave, my brother-in-law, talked with Kaye about delaying it. He didn't think I should have a skin graft so soon after surgery. He felt that the doctors should leave the wound to begin to heal on its own, as I could get an infection from all that poking and removal of my skin for grafting. Also, this would be very painful for my legs and buttocks.

Kaye's journal had the following entry:

> Now there is much discussion with family about closing the wounds. We are so unsure as to what to do. Up until this time, we were dealing with the aftermath of George's surgery and the days he spent in ICU. But now we have the unknowns of when and how to close wounds-cadaver coverings, skin grafts, burn unit, infection ... it's so much to think through in a short period of time and discuss without George's help. And added to all that, since

leaving ICU, George has begun to tell details of the accident; thankfully, if there is a delay in closing his wounds it will give us some "breathing" time to begin the process of healing. In all this, I feel the presence of the Holy Spirit engulfing me and going before me, protecting me.

The night before surgery, Kaye called the head nurse and asked what the procedure was prior to surgery. She said, "The plastic surgeon talks to the patient and a significant other about the procedure."

Kaye replied, "I am the significant other, but the surgeon hasn't spoken to me, and I have questions. We want to delay the surgery and talk with the surgeon in my husband's room in the morning."

They prepped me for the operation on Sunday evening. That meant no water for twelve hours. Until that time and throughout the thirty-nine days of the first hospital, I was so thirsty. Some nights I would drink about four pints of water. (I guess all the morphine had something to do with that.) (See Kaye's journal, appendix 8.)

Kaye arrived at the hospital on Monday morning and approached the nurse's station to speak with the head nurse. "Can I help you?" she asked.

"Yes," Kaye replied. "I talked with the head nurse last night and told her we want to delay the surgery in the morning and want to talk with the doctor up in George's room."

"We gave him your message," responded the nurse, "and he said he didn't have time to come up and talk to you. Surgery is scheduled for 10:45. George will be down on the first floor, ready to go into surgery, and the doctor will talk to us then."

Kaye said, "There will be no surgery today."

With a look of disbelief on her face, the nurse asked, "You want to stop the surgery?"

"Yes," Kaye answered.

Hesitantly, she replied, "I will tell the doctor."

Within ten minutes, a frustrated and unhappy plastic surgeon came up to our room. He sat down on a stool right next to my bed. He did not acknowledge my wife and two daughters, who were sitting across from him. He talked to me about how he would try to pull the open wounds back together; he might have to use skin grafts from my body. Because the wounds covered so much area, the plastic surgeon said it would take quite a bit of skin to cover them. He would take skin from my thighs, lower back, hips, and bottom to cover the leg wounds. Closing the wounds would take a lot of my skin, a big area. It would not go perfectly, and moving my legs would be detrimental with a skin graft. I would have to stay immobile to a certain extent. At the donor site, an infection could occur where the skin had been taken from the person's body (second-degree burn). It usually takes seven to ten days for the area to heal. A major risk is an infection. Because the wounds covered so much area, the plastic surgeon said, "Honestly, it's a big decision."

I had stopped having water for twelve hours before the operation. I was more than thirsty. The doctor did not look at Kaye when he was talking to me. When the doctor wouldn't look her in the eye, it told me that he didn't like to be told he was wrong.

Kaye said there would be no operation. She was convinced that we needed a different doctor because of the plastic surgeon's demeanor and his explanation of the procedure to begin closing the wounds.

Her doubts were confirmed by remembering earlier discussions with Dave, our brother-in-law who is a dermatologist, about procedures and risks of closing the wounds at this time. Kaye wanted a different doctor and a second opinion, and I was in complete agreement with her. Kaye is not normally a fighter. She stopped this because God was speaking, and she listened, and it made a tremendous difference for the better outcome! She was intentional in changing the course of treatment. By God's sovereignty, there was no operation. I told the nurse to give me some water.

Dave gave us the name of another plastic surgeon. When Dr. Kubalak came in the afternoon, we asked to have a second opinion and to schedule an appointment with Dr. Abdullah. Dr. Kubalak told us there was a very high chance of amputation below the knee for both legs. (See Kaye's journal, appendix 9.)

> Dr. Kubalak, General/Vascular Surgeon, Meritcare, Consult, Skin Graphs, May 10—We asked if the wounds could be left to heal on their own. He answered, "If we don't cover the wounds to get them biologically sealed, they will not be manageable outside the hospital. As deep as the wounds are, it would take up to six months to heal on their own."

> With skin grafts, the wounds would be covered. If we wait several weeks, there will be less skin taken from George to graft. There is no advantage to do that. In 3–6 weeks after the skin grafts heal, George's legs would be protected from infection.

> The fasciotomy surgery will not affect the function of George's legs in the long run, even with the grafts. The tissue is viable, which means no amputation now. The longer we wait, the better the chances

of not amputating above the knees but having an amputation done at a functional level.

Craig and Marlen, our sons-in-law, had bought a disposable camera at my request. When the nurses were changing the bandages and my wounds were exposed, I asked one of them to take pictures of my legs. Based on her reaction to my request, she was probably thinking, *Why would you want photos?* "This is real," I said as I handed her the camera. (Photos are at the end of the book.)

The doctors continued to monitor my open wounds.

During that time, Dr. Klava, a rehab doctor, came to check my legs and feet. He tapped on them with his little hammer. He drew a line with his hammer handle up the bottom of my right foot, and I just about went to the ceiling from the sensation. The same thing happened with the left foot. Dr. Klava said, "Good. We have something to work with." That was another answer to our prayers.

A board was placed on the bottom of my feet to keep them straight, or the muscle (cords) would tighten fast. It hurt when the doctor pulled my foot back.

I had lost all ankle function, and I had foot drop, meaning I could not lift up the front of my foot. Dr. Klava said my nerves were like a telephone cable. The outside of the cable wasn't broken, but the inside was pinched off. Nerves heal at the rate of one inch per month. It was thirty-two inches from where my legs were pinned down to my toes. That meant thirty-two months to recover.

As the doctor examined my legs, he was encouraged by my quads in the upper leg. "All is very encouraging. Walk on these legs with a little bracing. The calf muscles will continue to regain function. They have been a concern, but if tissue continues to heal, looking good."

I had to move every two hours to prevent bedsores. Dr. Klava said, "Way ahead of the game where we were several days ago. Key was tissue survival." Before he left the room, I told Dr. Klava the story of my accident.

CaringBridge, Wednesday, May 12, 2004 11:21 PM CDT—Dad calls the little rubber hammer a "tomahawk." When Dr. Klava ran it up the bottom of his feet, Dad said it felt like Dr. Klava stuck his foot in a 110-volt socket! Thanks to all who have come to visit. Dad gains so much from your phone calls, thoughts, and prayers. He said today after Dr. Klava was in to see him, "He (God) is healing me." He sure is!

Physical and occupational therapists continue to see Dad once a day. They work him until he almost breaks a sweat.

Dad has been staying very busy with dressing changes, which take 30–45 minutes, twice a day. Dad basically teaches each new nurse what they have to do because each wound dressing is different. Dad definitely knows the routine by now! The nurses do appreciate his help.

His leg strength is about the same, and his kidneys are still stable. Keep praying Dad will not get infection and that his legs will continue to heal rapidly. Then he will only have to use as little as possible of his own skin for grafting.

Dr. Abdullah, the plastic surgeon, came for a consultation. He looked at the open wounds on my legs.

Dr. Abdullah, Plastic Surgeon, Plastic Surgeon Institute, Fargo, Initial Consult, May 12—Trained in a burn unit. Does mostly cosmetic surgery. Serious injury. Done well considering what it could have been-usually amputation. Two main concerns-infection and rejection. Can close some wounds but some wounds are too big to close with just the skin. Skin graft absolutely appropriate thing to do. Wound sizes are comparable to a 20–25% burn. Timing-when to do it. How? Walk a tight rope with timing of it. Wait long enough to cover the least amount. Swelling is going to stay as long as it's open. THE PLAN: Use cadaver and George's skin. Do cadaver skin here and then to Regions Hospital in MLPS and get started with grafting. This is a big deal. Do it at a university hospital because plastic surgery residents can watch all the time. Then under the care of a doctor who will be coming from there to Fargo in July. Can continue with him there.

In the course of the conversation, we told him we very much wanted him to be my surgeon. Dr. Abdullah said, "Yes, I would be happy to take care of you. And one thing, if I'm going to do it, we have got to do it right, or we don't do it. Have you taken a shower yet?"

"No, I haven't been out of bed for eight days."

At the time, I was receiving wet-to-dry dressings twice a day. From now on, I would have a new type of dressing change twice daily and would be taking a daily shower. The doctor ordered a Dakin's solution of one-fourth strength Clorox with a buffer to be put on the wounds twice a day to clean them up, keeping the bacteria in balance and getting the wounds ready for surgery. The dressing change would also involve using silver wound pads to help draw out the bacteria. He would use cadaver skin grafts and try not to use a skin graft from me. He didn't know if that would be possible, but he would try.

Dr. Abdullah said, "The hospital is the worst place you can be with open wounds because of infection, but it is the only place you can be." These were not necessarily words of reassurance for me.

Once a day, I would take a shower. The plan was to examine the wounds for a while to see what he was dealing with, see how much could be closed, and cover the remaining wounds temporarily with cadaver skin and then eventually skin grafts from me.

It was day eight in the hospital, and I hadn't been out of bed once. They scheduled me for a shower that evening. I hadn't even been moved from my bed to a chair, much less taken from my room to the shower stall down the hall! But I had good upper-body strength, so when I transferred myself from my bed to the shower chair, it was easy enough. Three nurses assisted with moving my legs, and down the hall we went. One of them asked me if I could transfer myself to the shower bench. "Sure," I said confidently. Remember—I'm the independent farmer guy who can do it!

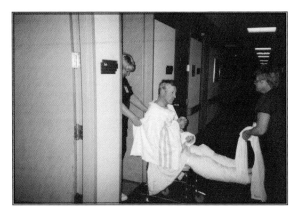

Shower time. Refreshing, but my legs really ached afterward.

So I moved from the chair to the shower bench. Well, this was the first time in eight days that my feet touched the floor, and because of the loss of blood to my brain, I fainted like a ton of bricks. The head nurse hit the alarm button, lifted me back into the chair, and soon I had six nurses around me. She saw I was breathing right away, so she knew I was all right. When I came to, I asked, "Are we done?"

"No way!"

And about my fainting, I told her, "Well, what do you expect? I've never been in a shower with three nurses before!"

They asked me if I still wanted to take a shower. I said we might as well as long as we were there. The following day, Teresa Nygard, the RN who picked me up off the shower room floor, wrote this on the message board in my room: "Have a non-adventurous day today!" Needless to say, my daily showers were not so eventful from then on.

> Dr. Kubalak, May 15—"When the dressings are changed, what causes the smell?" asked Kaye. Dr. Kubalak, "The odor is from what they put on it. There is a little drainage. There is some mucous. I want to clean it up and either change the Dakin's solution or strengthen it. Legs can be up in a chair. You can sit for a short period in a recliner."

> May 17—Very good for taking a graft. Wound assessments: Upper part—get together directly. Decrease size of another significantly. Lateral ones, not too much together. Inside thigh-bring together. Looking really good. Nurse: How do you attach a skin graph? Dissolvable glue or suture.

> May 18—Will do skin grafts with cadaver skin and
> pull some together. Trying to schedule surgery for
> this week.

As the doctor was leaving the room, he smiled and said, "Have a good day." It is the first time Kaye and I saw him smile.

Kaye's journal entry from May 19 follows:

Elizabeth & I left went home for a few hours today. We stopped at the vet clinic in Cooperstown to get West Nile virus serum and Frontline for our dogs, Pacer and Casey, and then got the house keys from Evelyn. Leon stopped by. We looked at the tractor and saw the crushed seat and broken hydraulic gear. Leon was amazed at how high the truck got. He had picked up the pencil and put it in the truck and told us that George has water jugs in every vehicle! The Dakota Central coffee mug was sitting on the hood of the tractor where I left it. I had used it to get water for George before going to get Dennis. We looked at the skid marks in the grass caused by the truck pushing the tractor until the truck engine quit. Leon helped plant squash, George's favorite vegetable and helped find the branding iron. He brought the deer license forms and said if George doesn't fill them out, he will! People ask him all the time about George. They copy Caringbridge at the café in Kensal. It's widespread-everywhere. It was so good to go home and have Elizabeth with me. She was a huge help. When we got back to the hospital, Elizabeth talked about the markings on the tractor tire where the truck went up. George responded, "It came up so fast, in an instant-like the snap of your finger. I put the tractor in neutral, thinking the truck would bump the tire, and it would stop."

> Dr. Kubalak, May 20—George is strong. He believes
> the surgery will go well tomorrow.

I had open wounds for seventeen days, with no infection.

In addition to the successful medical treatments and monitoring procedures used during this time to prevent infection, another effective prevention would be that all people washed their hands before entering the room. However, there was no way to know if medical staff and visitors were doing this. In addition, there were other occurrences that could contribute to bacteria contamination. One happened when Paige, our two-year-old granddaughter, threw up while she was eating an orange, and another was a frequent visitor who wanted to help me in some way. He would set up the food items on my tray until I explained the danger of infection and asked him to stop. Because of my doctor's concerns and research that shows "there is a high risk of infection in crush and deep structure wounds," I believe that God protected me from getting infection (https://ce.mayo.edu/sites/ce.mayo.edu/files/S_34_Boie-HighRiskWounds.pdf, "High Risk Wounds: Clinical Pearls").

During the first surgery to close my wounds, Dr. Abdullah was able to sew up five of the eight wounds and covered the rest with cadaver skin. All were closed on my right leg, and about one-third of them were closed on my upper left leg. The surgery took three and a half hours. The skin was pulled and held together with sutures. The doctor was very excited about how well the surgery went. He said, "George did very well." However, I had lots of pain. It was the most pain I had had since being in the hospital. The nurses set up a machine so I could push a button when I needed morphine. If there was a signal, I would receive morphine. If there was none, then it would be too soon, and I would try again. It was calibrated so it would give me only so much at a time.

> CaringBridge, Friday, May 21, 2004 6:20 PM CDT—George continues to drink water just about all of the time! When he was in the recovery room,

he drank five to six glasses and could hardly wait for ice water when he came back into the room. His sense of humor is still intact, and to that he has added vocals. As the nurses started to wheel him out of recovery, he began singing, "On the Road Again" only to be joined by the voices of other patients! We do not have the words to thank you for all of the support and prayers you have given us, but we do know that from great pain can come great joy, and we are beginning to experience some of that joy as we go through this. Kaye

2nd Surgery, Plastic Surgeon, May 24—Following this two-hour surgery, the doctor had a big smile and was very pleased. So much healing has taken place since last Friday! Several times Dr. Abdullah repeated, "It will be a long road for you with physical therapy and recovery." Dr. Abdullah said that he himself could not get through something like this. "George will set his mind to it and will do it," replied Bev. Dr. Abdullah, "He is an intelligent man, and that will get him through." The doctor won't start skin grafting until the other wounds are healed. He doesn't want seepage from small areas, here and there.

I was taken to a sterile environment (operating room) when the doctor determined it was necessary to change the dressings. The wounds looked healthy, with no signs of infection. Once, after I had returned to the room from a dressing change, Kaye met a nurse in the hall carrying two pitchers of water to my room. "Now he's using two pitchers at one time," she said, laughing.

Lee, a staff worker who brought my meal tray at noon each day and had a farm background, felt bad for me. In the course of one conversation, he said, "When I have a day off, maybe I could help out." Several days later as he was making his rounds to pick up empty trays, he came into my room, picked up my tray, and, standing in the doorway, sang in a warm, pleasant voice, "There's Room at the Cross," The chorus ends with these words: "Though millions have come, there's still room for one, Yes, there's room at the cross for you." Lee finished by extending an invitation to us. I thanked him for sharing this message with us.

Teresa Nygard, the nurse who picked me up off the floor in the shower, said she had been praying for me. One night, she was going to call at midnight, but she couldn't get through. She had Bible verses that she wanted to share with me. Teresa's new message on the board the next day was "His strength is made perfect in weakness."

> Consult, Plastic Surgeon, May 25—The wounds that are left to close are wide. The surgeon possibly could close the medial wound. The doctor doesn't think that the lateral wound can be closed, "but stranger things have happened." George said he has performed a miracle. The doctor said, "God does miracles; we just do the work."

> It will be important for the medial wound to be closed with sutures because a lot of George's skin will be needed for the lateral wound (they will start taking skin graphs tomorrow), and he might not have enough. The doctor didn't know what he would have done if the area had been huge. Kaye, "The pace of healing?" The doctor, "Better than average, faster than normal! What his wounds were like two weeks ago and what has happened in the last two weeks is

almost unbelievable. It's major that one leg is totally closed. The dressings can be taken off, and we do not have to deal with many open wounds on that leg. It will take one week for the sutures to hold and know that they will heal OK." When Kaye asked George how his spirits were, George said, "Good." The doctor said to George, "You have a lot of support," and then he looked at Kaye and said, "That's what counts at the end of the day."

3rd Surgery, Plastic Surgeon, May 26—With both arms, the doctor motioned to Kaye and Bev for them to come into the conference room. He closed up the medial wound! Smiling and laughing, he became more animated as the conversation went on. Yet, he doesn't think he can bring the last open wound together. Kaye said, "Stranger things have happened!" Later, the doctor admitted, "I'm going to miss these reporting sessions, but I don't want this to continue either!"

I was sitting up as the nurses were taking me down the hall to surgery in the transport bed. One of them said, "Patients like you make nursing well worth it, and your wife is nice too."

At the farm, the cows were being taken out to pasture the next day, as it was muddy in the feed lot. I ate heavenly strawberry pie from Grandma Dee's kitchen. In my prayer that day, I thanked God that Kaye and the kids had helped me so much spiritually and that Kaye wouldn't get too overwhelmed from the pressure.

Consult, Plastic Surgeon, Friday, May 28—Another surgery is scheduled for tomorrow morning. The plan is to hopefully pull some skin together and in a later surgery, to start the skin grafting. The doctor doesn't think he can do it without skin grafts, but "stranger things have happened." Because George has drunk so much water during his hospital stay, Kaye wondered if that helped to speed up healing. "Not really," answered Dr. Abdullah. "Is this a typical fasciotomy with the skin spread so far apart?" asked Kaye. "Yes." He continued on, "I haven't done something like this for a long time. I did have a similar case (crush injury) that ended in amputation below the hips."

4th Surgery, Plastic Surgeon, May 29—Half of the last wound (1" x 4") has been covered with cadaver skin. The doctor, with lots of smiles, laughing, exhilaration, and dancing eyes said, "It's very cool." Elizabeth replied, "We are just amazed at how rapidly his legs are healing, and you are able to pull so much together." Dr. Abdullah, "All we can do is say 'Thank you,'" as he looked toward the heavens with his hands held up in the air. "Things have happened fast."

The doctor is thrilled and amazed how fast the cadaver skin is adhering and vascular regrowth is starting; veins are starting to grow into the tissue. Dr. Abdullah usually just rips off cadaver skin but this has already started to attach.

When he does things, he likes to do them perfect. He is not as happy with the results this time because he had wanted it to come all together, but he played it safe. He pulled the skin together but didn't want to do it all the way to compromise the tissue and blood flow by stretching the tissue too much. If the tissue that he pulled doesn't do well, he can cut that away and take a little skin for grafting. George would be back into surgery in 3–4 days and a skin graft would be done. Then he would go home for 1–2 months to allow the skin graft to heal. During that time, the dressing would be changed once a week.

The next day, the doctor changed dressings in a sterile environment on the left leg. He looked to see if tissue was a good color as he doesn't want it to be purple. It is a desirable color.

On day thirty-two, June 4, Dr. Abdullah performed the last operation. Praise the Lord! He did all of the surgery without a skin graft from me. Dr. Abdullah, smiling, announced, "All done. All closed up."

We said, "You performed a miracle."

He looked up, pointed his finger to the ceiling, and said, "No, He did."

As I was brought back into the room, another nurse said, "He's been singing down there."

Kaye asked, "What song?"

The nurse answered, "'Somewhere Over the Rainbow.'"

Yes, I was singing. There were a number of people in the recovery room. The nurse had told me the results of the surgery. One more milestone! Elation!

> 5th Surgery, Plastic Surgeon, June 4—The 1" x 4" strip on the lateral side of left leg has been closed. Kaye said, "You have done the right thing to wait

and not be in a hurry to get things done." The doctor said, "Yes, it gave the tissues time to soften and be able to pull them together. George is doing fine." The doctor will bring George back to OR in a couple of days to change his dressings and then take the stitches out sometime soon.

I called each of the kids, my sisters, Kaye's folks, and Pastor Lori to tell them the news. It was the start of a beautiful day! When I came out of surgery, there was no sick feeling or anything. I was a little less drugged up on morphine and had a little bit of a thought process. I was ready to get to rehab and start doing something. I was ready to dance! No skin grafts. It was God's answer to prayer.

Two days later, the doctor took the dressing off my left leg. It looked good! I could start taking showers, sit up in a chair, and have the catheter taken out. Five surgeries in two weeks! My wounds were all closed up. No skin graft needed to be taken from me. No infection. Dr. Abdullah's initial projection that it might take months took God two weeks to accomplish. I felt great! I had not expected that a miracle would happen, but I did believe that things would work out regardless of the time frame. The only thing that got us over each hurdle successfully was prayers. It was awesome. God showed His power. There is nothing impossible with God. Praise the Lord!

# Leg Views With Sutures

## June 6, 2004

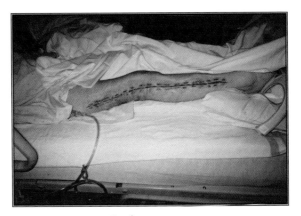

Right exterior.

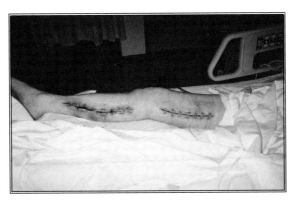

Right interior.

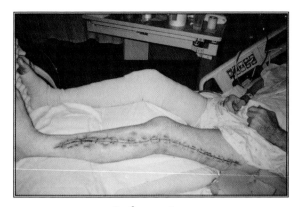

Left exterior.

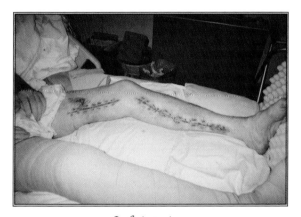

Left interior.

June 8—Doctor Kubalak will be meeting with some doctors. Possible start some rehab tomorrow. Never would have thought the wounds could be pulled together when he saw it first. Made him a believer in what Dr. Abdullah could do. Pleased with progress. Have no doubt what George can do when he gets into rehab. June 10—Off the case. Dr. Klava rehab doctor, takes over. We thanked him for what he has done.

I averaged more than a dozen visitors a day, and I told my story about turning everything over to God while being pinned on the tractor to many who came to see me. Muriel and a friend told me that I should write a book so that I could share my story with others.

One day, our daughter Liz brought a voice recorder to the hospital so I could ramble into it. Many mornings, I would wake up early and put my thoughts on the tape. One morning, when Kaye came in, I told her, "I know what the title of the book will be: *My Walk in Faith*." It still brings tears of thanksgiving to my eyes as I write this today, March 16, 2005. I'm very humbled and thankful. God never wastes a hurt. He has a greater plan, a purpose for my life after going through something like this. I'm determined to share my testimony so people can hear and see what God did and give Him the glory.

While I waited for my sutured wounds to heal before I was transferred to the rehab hospital, I visited a friend, Nate. Nate, who had been in the hospital a little longer than I, had had his stomach stapled. There was infection, which was draining into his belly. He was a very sick man and was very down about getting better.

Nate was really worried that he couldn't get timely things done while he was in the hospital. There was one thing I knew I had to do. I would try to help him and show him that there was still hope.

The night before I went to see him, I didn't sleep well. I didn't know what I would tell him. I prayed for an hour, searching for answers. Up until that point in my life, I had never prayed for an hour. This is something I'm not very proud of now.

The next day, I was able to go out of the room by myself in a wheelchair and wheel myself down the hall to see him. This was the first time I had left the room by myself in a wheelchair. I was not walking yet, but this was progress.

I told Nate how my neighbors came over and seeded soybeans and barley for me and how we couldn't be worried about what there was to be done at home. We just had to concentrate on getting better. I said that we are all replaceable; those jobs would get done even if we weren't there. We just had to trust the Lord that they would get done.

Well, the next day, I wheeled down to see him again. I didn't mention one thing about getting better. All I talked about was baseball and basketball. It happened to be dinnertime, and his sister came into the room with her food from the cafeteria. My friend introduced his sister to me, and he told her we were on the county weed board together. She asked, "Well, what did you talk about? Weeds?"

"No," he said. "We put that on the back burner for now."

Instantly, my mind lit up like a lightbulb; just maybe my message from the day before touched him. Helping a friend in need is like praying for him. There is so much satisfaction in it. He was in the hospital more than 180 days throughout the year, but he is back to work now. Praise the Lord!

Julie, a registered nurse who worked only on weekends, was another special person with a heart of gold. I told her my story, and it really touched her heart. She also told me about some of the difficult things that she had experienced. It was a very heart-wrenching story, but she had the strength from God to do the right thing.

She told me she would paint a picture for me. The day before I moved to rehab, she gave me the picture she had painted. It was Christ's nail-pierced hand with the verse of Isaiah 41:10 (NIV), "Fear you not; for I am with you: be not dismayed; for I am your God: I will strengthen you; yes, I will help you; yes, I will uphold you with the right hand of my righteousness." I'm thankful for her in my life.

The hand of Jesus reaching out to me.

On June 11, I was scheduled to change hospitals. I had been receiving physical and occupational therapy every day since leaving the ICU. All PT exercises were for my legs, as I had very good upper-body strength to transfer from my bed to a chair. The therapy consisted of knee bends, legs lifts, and moving my legs from side to side. Soon, however, I would be going to rehabilitation at the south university site.

The day before transferring, the physical therapist told me she would take me downstairs to rehab and have me stand along the parallel bars so I would know what it would be like to stand on my legs again and what I would be facing in rehab as I regained strength. I had not put any weight on my feet since the accident on May 3. I was still taking morphine and Darvocet A-500 for the pain.

Up until then, I had told everyone that I was ready to go to rehab, so "Let's get on with this." Well, that morning, I woke up full of anxiety and fear. I had been safe in my own routine. Now I was facing the unknown. We went down to the parallel bars. I stood there for three seconds and then said, "I have to sit down now so I won't faint." I stood again. This time it was for twenty seconds. Tomorrow it would be longer.

The first surgery to close my wounds was May 21, and the last surgery was June 4 (two weeks later). Most of the wounds had healed for three weeks, but the last wound had healed for only one.

# Rehabilitation

The first day in rehab was June 11. The physical therapist got me to the parallel bars for standing, and I stood for a few seconds, holding onto the parallel bars with my arms. My feet touched the floor just before I sat down. I stood again and this time put weight on my feet. The physical therapist asked, "How did it feel?"

I answered with a question, "Whose feet are these?

PT: "You don't know which way your feet are pointed. You can't sense where they are. Point your toes like they are pigeon-toed." I really worked hard at moving them. Then I looked down. My feet were straight.

The following morning, I walked fifteen feet. I felt like a new man. I used my arms to support 90 percent of my weight on the bars. That afternoon, I was able to walk thirty feet. The following day, sixty feet. The next day, I progressed to the walker and made it ninety feet. On day four, I was given air cast braces for my ankles, and I was able to go 160 feet without stopping. Throughout the time I was in rehab, I made steady progress, and at no time while I was walking was there any pain in my feet. I had stopped taking morphine after the second day there.

I made a pledge to myself that during rehab I would do everything the PT nurse asked me to do. I conveyed that to Kaye. I was on exercise machines, and the rehabilitation of walking progressed steadily. I learned how to go up and down steps with the walker and with crutches. However, I was concerned about the numbness and coldness I was feeling for the first time in my left foot. Would I lose my feet? The charge nurse assured me that sometimes it is a natural sign of healing. This was encouraging.

Later, I said, "It feels so good to feel the muscles in my knees just working. Everything is beyond the expectations of mine and the nurses. They just smile and shake their heads like this is something fun to observe: the willingness, ability, and sheer determination that I do the things they ask me to do."

Continuing, I admitted that my feet were not always in the most fluid motion because of my sense of balance. But I told the nurses I was willing to listen in order to do the proper technique, if I was able, and it would be done with the joy of feeling my muscles being exercised in the stepping. I felt the muscles in my thighs and knees only because I didn't have much feeling below my knees. I could sense that they were strengthening with every move I made. "Do you really believe that?" Kaye asked.

"Yes, I do! Don't get me wrong; this is not easy. This is hard work, but it is happening with the strength that I get from above. It's a joy to be with people who know how to stretch me to the limit without doing damage to my muscles. They are genuine, knowledgeable, patient, and caring. They are a gift from God, and I have much confidence in them. I am totally refreshed right now after talking with a cousin and a friend and just waiting to face a new day because I know my recovery is one day at a time."

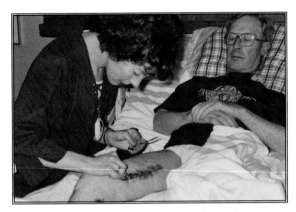

Stitches out. Six young nurses came to learn how to remove stitches. They had never seen it done before because staples are usually used. The area tingled when the stitches came out.

I was using a tape player and was thrilled with the therapy of talking on tape whenever I woke up in the middle of the night or during the day. (It was so helpful and great.) "I feel as rested after talking into the tape as if I took a thirty-minute nap!" It had a calming effect on me. It relieved tensions when I could vent about a problem and brought me joy when I was happy about something. I felt refreshed and stronger emotionally, supported and listened to, less alone.

Excerpts from the audiotaped journal follow:

> June 16—I'm reading a little handout that Kaye got from the church service. It says your identity comes from what God has done, and I cannot, I cannot have the attitude that says I did it, I'm the only one. It's just beyond me to say that because I know I get the strength from Him. Your identity, also, comes from what people say about you. I know it is going to be totally different as I speak to my friends, and I might have little self-doubts that say, "Well, he talks a good talk." But it's totally what God says about

me that matters. It's just what I want to point out at this time.

This morning was the most physical workout I have had to date. They put extra strain on my muscles above my knees. It was … just really … a test of physical endurance and there wasn't any pain, but I did have a series of lightheaded feelings where I had to sit down. The extra stress was caused mainly from doing deep knee bends and mainly keeping my knees flexed more as I walk so they do not hyperextend.

When I woke up from my nap, I had to go to the bathroom ever so dearly. I put my light on. I waited about two minutes, started out, and I decided I'm not going to wait any longer. The nurse had not come. I shuffled over, got in my chair, and as I opened my bathroom door, I looked out the door, and there were three nurses talking and chuckling to each other, laughing and having a conversation, so I proceeded to go to the bathroom. When I was in there, Jen came in, the nurse, and I had to tell her that I was frustrated at the time. Just a point of frustration … I jump off the handle a little bit but about the … it set me off when they were laughing and chuckling and they didn't come to my call. So I made an agreement with her. I will put my light on, and at least they will be on the way if I have to do the shuffle and the exchange by myself, which I'm, I feel very capable and confident of doing. She agreed with me. Today is a good day.

I'm just reading about the county fair that is coming up, and I will most definitely be there on the night of the hymn sing. It is something I'm looking forward to … to publicly thank all my friends for their support and prayers. My plans are I am going to sing the song *Amen,* so I'm going to have to learn that and be accompanied by a piano. It's just one of the first public announcements that I have for my Lord and Savior.

June 17—Last night I took a shower. The nurse and I were down at the end of the hall, and we had an interesting experience with the showerhead. The water pressure is so variable when they flush toilets, it goes from cold to just about too hot, which is a very dangerous situation. We end up just using a basin to take the shower, and then we report this to the nurses. This afternoon after PT, I plan on taking a shower, and this evening, they will be taking us to the movies. We will plan on going. They're going to even give us popcorn.

Just came down the hall from OT. Met Art Johnson from Ottertail. He used to be a chaplain. And ah, well, I said, coming to the intersection, I said, "You have to look both ways, you know at these intersections." He was right there, and he was chuckling. So we started talking, and he gave me a message … I told him my story and how helpless I was and the great sense of peace that came over me when I said, "Thy will be done." And ah, I told him my wife has usually been with me every time I tell this story to everybody. She has been my rock.

He continued to tell me a few things. I was saying we are never to judge somebody about his faith or lack of faith, because we are not to judge. (I had been concerned about what my friends at home might think of my transformation, that they might not believe it to be true.) He laughed, and he said, "Hey, you know that reminds me of a story. A man came to a holy man and asked him how he could become more like him. The holy man said, 'You don't know the pain and suffering I had to go through to become this way. Don't set your sights on me, but set them on God because all of us humans will fall short, at one time or another.'"

Also, he was ever so pleased to hear my message, and he mentioned that his wife is, I believe, a quadriplegic. And ah, I greeted him later by saying, "I will pray for your wife." And hopefully I will meet this man again. And I told Art Johnson I would forever tell this story to anybody that stops long enough to listen and to proclaim His name, and ah, there was you might say a connection. Just ah ummm a very, very warm feeling. And I will never quit proclaiming this, it's ah, it's being ever so thankful.

Kaye and I were talking about the hunting trip I went on with Ron and Don Wagonner and Jeff Topp. She was talking about how we made a connection. And I was telling that they were reading scriptures one evening, and Don give me the Bible and asked me, "Would you like to read this passage here?" And I read it, and I don't remember what it was. But the next morning and other mornings as we'd go out hunting, they would pray aloud as they were on horseback, and I did too, but it was at that point in my faith it was more of a tagalong. It was just that one step on a journey.

I'm ready to go down to OT and PT, it's about one o'clock, but I have to read this passage from the calendar from Colleen. "This message was kept secret for centuries and generations past but it has now been revealed to his own holy people for it has pleased God to tell his people that the riches and glory of Christ are for you Gentiles, too. For this is the secret, Christ lives in you and this is your assurance that you will share his glory" (Col 1:26–27 NLT).

In PT, they put a pedal-like device in PT mounted at the base of my wheelchair that I pedaled at the end of PT for five minutes. Maybe I stopped thirty seconds in between. You could go forward and reverse, and man, what a workout. My legs are spent. Also, in PT, they put the air cast on my right foot, which was just a total 100 percent improvement for my walking. I made most of the circle with just one stop. And then I did some knee bends on the parallel bars with forward and backward motion.

It was much simpler in OT. We stop at a station where we have different pipe fittings, maybe a dozen or fourteen pieces of pipe, connections, Ts, and they show me a picture, and I'm standing beside my walker with the wheelchair behind me. But just to get my sense of balance as I stand, Dave, occupational therapist, has me put this puzzle … just put the pipes together by hand, don't tighten them to tight, and I alternate hands, grab one piece, screw it on, grab the other piece, screw it on, right or left hand. And continue to try to keep my balance, which I do very well.

We go over to the next table. There is a Hula-Hoop that is cut in the half. It is bolted on each end on the top of the table, so it's a loop, a half a loop, 180 degrees. On that are washers that are about four-inch-long plastic and then the hole in the center to facilitate that you move one washer up over the hoop, which is above your head, and down to the other side. So I move several with my right hand and come back and move several with my left hand.

Then we go to the pedal bars that you pedal with your hands, and today we stand up to the pedals, and he raises them up, and I'm standing when I pedal with my hands. The chair is behind me. I go to work three or four minutes on that. They have some resistance on it. Sense of balance is right there.

Anyway, I come back, and I get in bed. It is about two thirty. I don't get my pain pill till four o'clock. But after that workout, the bottoms of my feet … much burning sensation … they just kind of pain. I lay down. In a space of two minutes, my left foot … second and third toe … the ball of my foot … all just turn to a warm sensation. There is very little pain in my right foot, and it is just a sensation of relaxation. A sense of different feelings. Well, I'm totally elated.

My dear wife comes in, and I have to tell her that, with tearful eyes, that I know God is working. I continue to lay there, and the pain comes and goes just a little bit, different sensations, and I wait to possibly four o'clock, and I get my pain pills. I send Kaye off to take a nap. She's going down to OT on fourth floor into one of the rooms.

Kaye's journal had the following entry:

> When I came into the room, George was praying and then prayed with me. He held me close and cried like I've never seen him cry. He is just so grateful and blown away. He sees God in the things he reads, what people say, and what he tells others. He feels the presence of the Holy Spirit. I asked him to describe that for me. "It's like I have a friend walking beside me."

More excerpts from the audiotaped journal follow:

> Jess comes in to give me a shower. We did it with one pan of water, because we did not use the showerhead. She would rinse me off, and it worked just super. And in this time of my total elation, I'm talking to her and rambling on. I sense and I'm sensing this just to myself, but I'm thinking she just about has to think I'm at the point of craziness or just a little off the teakettle ... I guess my mannerisms, they are somewhat strange to myself by the way I am so expressive, the way I'm talking about things. It's total joy.

> I get back in bed. Then I put my lotion on and do my wraps for the very first time, and I call Jess back in and I said, "I was raving in there don't ask me why, but I can tell you I was not crazy. It was just

maybe the joy of these things when the pain goes away." And possibly added to that … I'm thinking about going to a show in the evening. They have it scheduled. They are taking us to a show. We are going to go to that show, and they are going to buy us popcorn.

Then I'm ready to go, and okay, I eat my supper. It's after six o'clock when Kaye said she would be back, and she's not here. So I get Jess and we go down to look for her. I roll down to fourth floor and go into OT. Jess looks in the one room, and no Kaye. Then she reaches for the next door. It's locked. "Well, Jess, the only other place she has to be is up at PT."

We go up to PT. Needless to say, we don't find her there. We go back down to OT, and Jess goes into the extra rooms and looks in this other bedroom. I am just about totally berserk. I told Jess, I said, "You gotta think I'm crazy now." Who walks in? Kaye. After she took a nap, she had gone to a computer (letting out a sigh, taking in a breath) … it was a … (clearing throat) it was quite a story, but we get back up here, we go to the show.

Going to the movies.

A few events there. Before leaving the hospital, a nurse slipped the urinal in the carrier behind my wheelchair, just in case I have to go to the bathroom. We get to the show hall. I don't see Kaye carrying anything. "Where's the urinal?" I speak out, and people are listening. I'm sure it embarrasses Kaye somewhat as we're talking. Kaye doesn't remember the nurse putting it back there. Someone said, "Well, maybe it's in the van," but they found it behind my wheelchair seat in the carrier.

We get our popcorn and pop and go down the ramp into the theater to see *Raising Helen*. The section for the wheelchairs is right at the first and second rows. I never go to a movie sitting that close to a screen. We watch it approximately five minutes, and I tell Kaye I have to get out of here. I can't keep my eyes even open to it because it is just (pause), it is getting me, getting me just dizzy.

Kaye said, "Well, we'll go over to *Shrek 2*." Well, we get to *Shrek 2*. I stop on the ramp on the side halfway down, and we start to watch *Shrek 2*. Maybe I'm eating my popcorn and drinking my lemonade. I maybe last ten minutes or fifteen minutes. I said to myself, "This is not working." I started to breathe heavily and felt some pressure on my chest. Kaye is sitting nearby on the other side of the guardrail bar.

Just at a quiet time in the movie, I holler out her name. She comes, and we go up to the entryway where I get some fresh air. I was very nervous and didn't know what was happening to me. I was desperate to keep my focus and not black out. Dustin, a young attendant, gives me some water, and I tell him I have to go to the bathroom. I splash cold water from the water fountain on my face and the back of my neck. Kaye took me outside for fresh air. I'm talking to the manager, and I tell the manager, "You have to keep talking to me so I can keep my focus," as they are in the process of getting the van driver, and finally I say, "You have to call 911." Kaye said, "They've already called for the bus driver." So we … we got in the van, and I continued to converse all the way home. As we leave the van, I do tell the bus driver I'm really okay. I can tell that.

We get here and into the bed, I lay down. I'm … I maybe … I would say … I'm in shock. I think I am having the big one, (heart attack) and Kaye is reading the Bible. They are trying to find Liz and Josh Burbank's number because that is where Liz and Craig are. Well, maybe within a half hour, Liz comes up here.

They give me a pill. They tell me to keep calm, and I try to slow things down. It's an anxiety attack. I did not lose any recollection of any conversation that I had, and as I was slowing down in my attempt, in my feeble attempt, to try to let them know that I was okay, I would make comments. One comment I told the nurse, "Did you know you are the only nurse that has the worst bad breath I've ever smelled." I mean, I'm sorry I ever told that to her, and later I said I was sorry. Also, while Kaye was reading the Bible, the shades were partly pulled. They had the lights off. It was hard for her to read. She would be reading, and she literally tore pages out of the Bible reading me Psalms. She would be reading, and she'd lose track of where she could see. She'd skip to another line, and I'd say, "You skipped some verses or skipped to another chapter." So, needless to say, my blood pressure got down, and at this point in time, I guess I won't be going home tomorrow, but that is all right. We will look forward to another day of good work. And with God's help, it is going to be a good day.

Saturday morning, June 19. Just happened to think. It's Topp Reunion today (yearly reunion of the Topp family held in Grace City). It is twenty minutes after six o'clock, and sleeping without a sleeping pill is a more natural sleep. It feels good not to use a sleeping pill. I was even dreamin'. It was in calving season, and I was running after the cows while getting them into the different pens for calving.

And just a prayer for this morning, "Our most gracious heavenly Father, don't let me get to such good physical ability that I will never be ever thankful. I want to keep thanking You, and I pray for my soul that I never let up. I am so thankful and look forward to each new day … all the new things that I learn with Your helping hand. Amen."

We met with Dr. Lund, a psychiatrist. He said that I had experienced a panic attack, and during a panic attack, at no time would any physical harm come to me. He told us there were no emotional concerns. I had responded to certain stresses and situations. He described panic attacks and what to do. All of this information was helpful to know.

We are going to talk with Dr. Klava about getting an overnight pass to go home. Dr. Lund said we should go home just to get a taste of things to come after my release. My mental state is at all times to think of … know my limitations on this day. And this is how I will be working things out every day or strive to do this.

The same day, I would be cooking in OT. I wanted to boil lutefisk, but the therapist didn't even entertain the idea! I opted instead for the next best fish, fresh walleye. I didn't get walleye. We ate chicken instead!

Going home on Father's Day weekend.

A very eventful day ... the homecoming ... for a visit.
Everything was back to our normal, so we asked the
doctor if we could go home. He gave us the okay, and
we left the hospital for the farm. We had so much
fun traveling, stopping here and there. A Saturday
summer day outing! Just west of Fargo, we smelled
skunk. I said, "Skunk never smelled so good!" I saw
all the foliage for the first time this summer, the
crops and all the water and the new construction of
Randy Stedman's house. However, the ride wasn't
easy for me. I had pain. I am weak, so I still can't
tolerate an excess of most things.

We got home about three o'clock. Jeff Edland and
Leon were finishing up spraying the soybeans. We
stopped on the road, and I have a very tearful and
joyous reunion with Leon. He comes up to the house
to help as I go up the steps. I went up the steps very
easily. We go inside, and who else shows up but is
another friend, Alan. Also when I met Leon, I said,
"Friends forever." With Dennis Hofmann, I have

three new brothers. It's such a joy to have a bond with them. Previous to this day, Alan came up to visit me one time in the hospital, and he said, "Friend." We shook hands and ahh, when he came today, he said today, "You know when I said friend to you, I remember the time when I went to a meeting and saw my friend from a business experience. He came up to me, and he said, 'Friend.'" Alan said, "I knew he meant it." I also said, "And I knew you meant this, Alan." I also told him when I met Leon, I said, "Friend forever." (See Kaye's journal, appendix 10.)

June 20. Father's Day. I got up this morning, and I made oatmeal for Kaye and myself just to get back into routine of things. I had Leon come over to trim that bush so we had clear sailing on the sidewalk. We went to church. I made it up the stairs inside the church with the walker, and I sat in my wheelchair behind the back pew. To listen to the words of Pastor Lori, it was so great. It was a good reunion with our church family. Donna Resler was there, also. She is my cousin from Seattle. Frank Lester was the first to tell me happy Father's Day, and I told him so. Later, I mentioned that to Kaye. She said she had forgot. Understandably so.

Just a short list of who was there at church this morning. Les and Colleen, Alf and Margaret, Tina, Jean House, Rod and Deb, Royce and Mary, Donna Resler, Vera Topp, Esther Scanson, Lisa Scanson, Kerwin and Flora Borgen and two grandkids, Roger and Phyllis. And we were led in worship by Pastor Lori. It was just a good homecoming, and her words of inspiration were so true to me. And I told her her sermon sounded like it lasted only five minutes.

The songs that we sang in church today were more than fitting for my thoughts ... "Jesus Is All the World to Me" and in the songbook, "More Like You." And the threefold amen after the Lord's Prayer. I think it's a new one they have been doing since the time of the accident. I don't remember it from before, but I know it. The last two hymns were "Have Thy Own Way, Lord" and "Wonderful Words of Life" ... such inspirational words with a deep meaning for me. (See Kaye's journal, appendix 11.)

We just had a good talk with Karen and Elizabeth, and as I look outside, I see numerous monarch butterflies going up to the lilac bush. Kaye brought up the observation about the anxiety attack. She is totally convinced it had nothing to do with my going home that evening, and I totally agree with her because never at any moment during that time of the evening when I was looking for Kaye and being anxious or when we were at the movies, never one moment did I ever think about me going home the next day. It just didn't cross my mind. So it just has to be in our mind, a 95 percent case of car sickness at the movies, and we will be conveying this to Dr. Klava.

Just a note of something to be concerned about. Earlier today, my concern was about Kaye. Maybe she is starting to reach a stress level. We were talking with somebody, and she was disagreeable. I said, "Maybe ... I think we will be going to Corey's," and she says, "Well, we'll just have to wait and see on that. We don't know. We'll have to wait until Tuesday." Maybe it was a case of the stress level … just something to think about. Hopefully it will pass. I pray for her.

Also, two other points. When I told her maybe we could leave at 9:30 p.m. and actually to get going earlier to get some sleep, she said, "I just have these things to do," which she does, but she kind of looked noncommittal maybe, and today she made a list for things to bring down. Then when she got down here, she said, "I never even looked at the list." So there's some articles we did forget, and that's just … forgetfulness is really not the concern right now.

Hospital room 11:50 p.m. It is very cold tonight in my room. Already now I had to go to the bathroom again. The nurse brought in extra blankets for me. I'll try to get back to sleep right now. If not, I'll have to be in contact with the nurses. My observation of this situation at 11:55, the heat is not working in this room, and I'm going to talk to the nurses. They have to put a thermometer in here to find out the heat or if it is my physical or mental state. When I'm laying here trying to go back to sleep, all I listen to is my heartbeat, thump, thump, thump, thump, thump, thump, so I think it is a bit elevated.

I had a nurse come in, Barb. I'm still cold. She puts the second heating blanket on me. Within two minutes, I'm just about sweating and starting to roll the covers back. I will keep you posted. The time is twelve thirty. I had a total of six covers on. Now

I am down to one cover. If I have the cover off, the air is too cold. But otherwise, with one cover, I'm too hot. I'm requesting a nurse to turn the heat down in the room. It's a very puzzling situation. I had the nurse turn the heat down to seventy-five in the room. I think they had it up to about seventy-nine previous to this … It must be a little bit warm. I do the dreaming that the doctors are coming in (swallowing) and they are torturing me. They say I have to have the legs … they don't deliberately say they are cutting them, but they have to be cutting them, they are on them, and it will hurt for two or three days. I know it's a dream. Very realistic.

June 22. I'm just going through this scripture journal book that Kaye gave me. I read every scripture on every page. They are so meaningful to me. It gives me peace, and hope, and a lack of fear. There's somewhat more tingling and hot and different sensations on the soles on my feet. But I know that's just the workings of my body as it is healing.

We had a very good series of workouts in PT and OT. We used the cane for the first time in the parallel bars, and we used the crutches with that arm support on the back of the arm for the first time. Obviously, the cane was not like the walker, but doing the four-point walk with the cane the first day, a little bit balance, and it will come. I used the canes to go up and down the steps, which it worked wonderful, and actually going up and down the steps is easier than that than walking with the walker. Played catch tapping a balloon back and forth with a cane, and having the cane on one arm and tapping with the other hand, continue to throw a ball that's on a string while we used the walker there. That was in OT throwing the ball, and it would swing back, and I would have to catch it.

We got back to the room about twenty to three, put signs on the door, and I was able to get an hour-and-twenty-minute nap, which is much needed for my physical state, and it was very good. I woke up. I was ready to take the pain pill, but there is more burning sensation on the bottom of my feet today than most other days, just because I was on my feet more today. The burning sensation has to be a good sign, you know. Burning is pain. There's feeling. It's all good signs.

June 23. Woke up this morning again at five thirty. I went back to sleep, and I slept longer. A very good sleep. As of last night about until six to seven o'clock and mostly throughout the night, and even right now, I do have more of a burning sensation all the way from the ball of my feet, at the base there, and up through my toes on both feet. I take it as a good sign because of the pain and having feeling there. Andrea and Paige came up. Paige brought me a dandelion.

June 24. A new day. New things to look forward to. My nurse is bringing ice water. Pam was in here at 2:00 a.m. putting my booties on, and needless to say, she didn't get out of here without me telling her the story also. She does have a heart of gold. I can see she was touched, and it is just one more little therapy for me maybe helping somebody. There is so much anticipation and joy to be saying I'm going home via a short trip to MLPS for the weekend to have a reunion with Karen and Corey and their families. I anticipate it's going to be a very relaxing weekend, plus a few little noises from the kids. And it's just, ah, I know we're going to have a very happy time.

I just put on my set of Jobsts ... five minutes for the first one and four for the next leg. I know it will get easier every day. Hey, this is departure day. With His help, I am ready. We will make it.

MJ was just in, and I talked a little bit with her, but she's too busy for me to tell her the story, but I am going to tell her before the day is up. And she is touched by just what I have accomplished and with the help of God. And I will be talking to her today, and, ah, I will be going down to see Nate today before we leave. We will have to work it in. Pam just came in and wished me well. She's off for the day. And MJ came back, and I was able to tell her my story. I'm just getting my shoes and clothes on, and I just marvel that I got over here on the tenth and it was on the thirteenth when I told my wife, "Nobody will put my shoes on again." My rehabilitation ... it's just been awesome. I have enjoyed every minute of it even though there has been work. And I'm just looking forward to the continued work as I go on to my recovery. It was quite a workout in PT today ... the ten steps up and down without any problem with Mom assisting. I am ready for a nap now and clear sailing towards MLPS.

(Later that evening.) We're in Albany, Minnesota, at a motel. The ride went very well. Mom and I talked more than we ever have in our life on a trip (long series of laughs, Kaye, too) ... and called Corey and let him know we would be there in the morning.

June 25. The trip through the cities went fine for Mom, as this is the first time she has driven here. It was a short ride, and the traffic was ... I would say normal. Got everything moved in and are taking it easy now. Corey came home from work and made lunch for us. We're going to have a nice quiet afternoon and get ready to see the little ones tonight.

Dr. Klava said I should be cutting back on pain pills, so I have started to do that. At no time was there pain in my feet when I was doing the strenuous work in PT. It would only be muscle fatigue, and actually today at Corey's, I have a pain in my feet. It's on the outside of my left foot, and it does not go away at this time as I walk. So you could say this is the first time I am walking with a little pain, but I think it's because of taking pills at six-hour intervals instead of every four hours.

Kaye read books to Ryan, Kyle, and Justin, and we played cards. Then I went down to the basement to take a shower. Corey helped me motivate the steps, and I worked up quite a sweat! I sat on a plastic lawn chair in the shower, and that's the best shower I have had in a couple months. (Chuckle.) I could have stayed in there all night!

June 26. It's 7:11 a.m. and I hear Justin yell out, "Daddy!" Karen and Tad and Barb and Dave got here about, oh one thirty or something like that, and we've been having a great time … just some heart-to-heart talks with everyone. A mouse scared Kyle when the boys, Corey, and Tad were playing football in the backyard. Tad chased it down and killed it. Corey, Karen, Tad, and I played pinochle later in the evening.

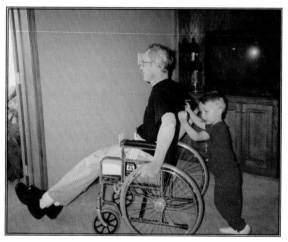

Justin: "I can help, Grandpa!"

The following afternoon, we left for home, stopping in Alexandria for the night. The next morning, we saw family in Fargo and picked up leg weights at K-mart. Then I went to Elizabeth's to take a nap. After about an hour or so, I wake up, and Mom and Liz are still shopping. Well, I decide, well, if I'm going to get upstairs, I'll have to do it. So I walk up the stairs with crutches and had no problem and totally confident of my ability and still keeping in mind I have to know my limits for the day. On the way home, I sat in the back seat of the car with my legs up most of the time. We did not have to stop so the rides are getting better. We made it home (it's so good to be home). Leon came and helped unload. I'm stretching out on the bed and putting some things away and resting a little bit. Took a shower. Water was warm. Leon must have turned it on.

I have a short report on the weekend that we spent at Corey's. I spent some very good times with Corey when I was alone with him during the weekend. I had some good talks with him. We talked about the farming situation, and what things we have to decide on, and the upcoming season and cash rent, working out cattle with somebody. I told him of the plans we had … Mom and I had talked about the week before. So it's whatever decisions we'll make, we hope we won't make them too hastily and have a fair settlement with anybody that is working for us or is doing shares of cattle or whatever. We look for guidance for that.

I was able to have a good talk with Karen. Just told her about my progress and maybe more so about the closeness Mom and I have attained, the spiritual closeness, and the similarities of things that come up, and just how we know that God is answering prayers. For instance, the picture that Julie painted has the verse Isaiah 41:10 (NIV) on it. Well, the kids had the painting framed and gave it to me as a gift for Father's Day. Well, the next morning, Mom and I were reading in the Upper Room, and for that date, it had reference to Isaiah 41:10 (NIV), and that was so touching. I really take it as a sign from above. It is just a rewarding feeling to get these signs … We know that our help is coming from above.

July 1. We went as planned to the hymn sing at the Foster County Fair. I had been a member of 4-H for ten years and a leader in 4-H for thirty years. I have a fondness for the fair and have sung in small groups at the hymn sing in previous years. I thought it was a good time to make a public appearance. So, that evening, we went for supper and then to the hymn sing. With help, I rolled my wheelchair to the edge of the wooden steps, stood up, grabbed my crutches, and maneuvered my body up the five steps to the platform. We surprised Deb Presser, hymn sing leader, as she didn't know that I was going to sing. Terry Lund said, "It's nice to have George Topp back with us." I sat down in my wheelchair and thanked everyone for their support, telling them I was very thankful for my recovery and I would never stop praising His name for my recovery. Kaye played as I sang the song, "Give Thanks with a Grateful Heart." After I finished, Ervin Swanson stood up and clapped.

"Give Thanks"

Give thanks with a grateful heart
Give thanks to the Holy One
Give thanks because He's given Jesus Christ, His Son
And now let the weak say, "I am strong"
Let the poor say, "I am rich
Because of what the Lord has done for us"
Give Thanks

# Healing at Home

"For I know the plans I have for you," declares
the Lord, "plans to prosper you and not to harm
you, plans to give you hope and a future."
—Jeremiah 29:11 NIV

On the morning of July 3, 2004, while at home, I continued to use the cane when I walked. I was making breakfast in the kitchen. It's about six feet from one counter across the room to the other. I looked at the counter and said to myself, "Let's see if I can make it." I walked across without a cane. When Kaye came out into the room, I said, "Look." I then proceeded to walk about eight feet to her without the cane. We shed tears of joy and thankfulness. Remember—I had to learn how to walk all over again. I then had a strong belief that I would see signs from God every month on or near the third of every month, the anniversary day of my accident. God did indeed surprise me with significant events on a number of those days.

Doctor Abdullah—return appointment, July 15, 2004.

CaringBridge, Sunday, July 18, 2004 2:38 PM CDT—George and I have been home for about three weeks. We are doing well. When George came home from the hospital, he was using a wheelchair, walker, and crutches. Today he uses only a cane and can walk through the house without it as long as there is something nearby with which to steady himself. He will be wearing new braces in about a month. Each brace will be one solid piece that extends from the back of his legs below the knees to the tips of his toes. Then he will be able to walk without a cane and drive the car.

George has mowed the yard several times, raked grass clippings, planted a tree, and rides the 4-wheeler wherever he wants or needs to go in the yard, fields, and pastures. He makes breakfast in the morning, helps with meals, and washes dishes.

Our neighbors and friends are in daily contact with us about current and future farm work. They are finishing a brief second round of spraying soybeans. The cattle are routinely checked in the pastures, and the hay is being cut, raked, and baled. The work they have done, and the work they continue to do, has been nothing short of inspiring. We are deeply grateful.

After one session of occupational therapy in Carrington, it was determined that George would no longer need OT; however, he has three one-hour sessions of rigorous physical therapy each week. In addition, he exercises daily using weights, rides the Air dyne bicycle, and takes a long nap in the afternoon.

Considering the seriousness of George's injury, and the length of time his legs were crushed and swollen, we could not have hoped for any better results from last week's EMG (Electromyography) and NCV (Nerve Conduction Velocity) tests performed by Dr. Klava. The most important result showed that the nerve that controls his ankle and foot is intact.

You have been and continue to be a blessing to us. Thank you once again for your prayers. We give all the praise and glory to God for what He has done and continues to do. Kaye

August. We needed to drive to Fargo for another EMG test; it tests the nerves and response time in my legs. Dr. Klava said, "I am cautiously optimistic you will get all of your muscle function back, but it might take three years." I told myself I would beat that time prediction with the help of the Lord. I got my permanent braces. I baled some hay and told Kaye we wouldn't have to rent the land out next year. I will be able farm.

September. When I first woke up, I looked at my feet. I said to myself, "Let's see if I can move my feet." Surprise! For the first time, I could move my right foot about one inch from side to side. I then moved both feet from side to side. I also moved my toes on my right foot.

October. I can walk without a cane, almost everywhere, at all times. When standing still, I can feel my balance transferring from my knees to my ankles. I went pheasant hunting with my son-in-law, Craig, and his dad, Lyle Bjur. I walked one-third of a mile at one time and close to one full mile on that hunt. At Jessi Black Johnson's wedding, I danced about twelve dances. I wasn't the most graceful, but it felt good. Remember that this was my goal—to be dancing at her wedding.

Dancing with Jessi (Black) Johnson, friend—October 2004.

November. On the first day of deer season, I didn't walk, just posted. Because I didn't wear compression stockings, my calves were swollen. I didn't sleep well during the night. I tossed and turned a lot. I had no pain, but my legs didn't feel just right. After that, I knew I needed to wear them. I combined soybeans and have been doing field work and hauling bales.

In all this time of working, I haven't had pain in my feet. Several times, yes, if I'm on them too long, but when I wake up in the morning, I have no pain then. I can do more with my feet all the time.

We sent a letter to Dr. Klava, the rehab doctor, asking him two questions. The first was, "What is the prognosis for someone who sustained the kind of injury that George had?" Dr. Klava: "Relatively remarkable recovery for that extent of injury. Anything gained at this time is a bonus." Second question, "It is unimaginable that anyone could endure that kind of pain for such a long a period of time. In relation to the pain, could you describe what was happening to George's body?" Dr. Klava said, "Beyond twenty minutes, cell and tissue damage. This is the reason that, up to a full week, we considered amputation. Amputation to save George's kidneys."

December. I have to tell this story. Seven months to the day of the accident, another sign came from God to us. We were in Fargo that day, and we were trying to decide where to eat our evening meal. We were going to the I Hop restaurant, and then at the last minute, we turned into the HuHot restaurant where Mongolian stir fry is the specialty.

When we walked in to sit down, we saw Dr. Kubalak, the doctor who performed the fasciotomy my first night in the hospital. He and his wife were dining there. Kaye and I walked over to his table. Remember—I had no braces on. He definitely remembered me, and he introduced us to his wife. I told him, from the first day out of ICU, I had total faith I would fully recover. He was the one who had the call on whether or not to amputate. His comment was, "Well, sometimes it seems I'm wrong more times then I'm right." His wife told us about a book that she had wanted to buy, *Amazing Grace for the Catholic Heart,* but it wasn't at the bookstore when she checked last.

We said our goodbyes and went to our table to eat. They left the restaurant shortly. Now, there was a bookstore right next door. Mrs. Kubalak came back into the restaurant to our table with the book that she had been looking for. She said, "The doctor asked me to buy this and give it to you; it was just meant to be."

January 2005. I went to New Rockford men's breakfast prayer group. I experienced no needles or tenderness in my heels, and I had started walking one and a half miles a day. I shared my story with the men's group. I enjoyed coffee with the Binford gospel singers at the Glenfield grocery. Later that day I walked one and a half miles. I even ran a little on the way back to the house for the first time. I thought, *That felt good!*

I went to rehab in Fargo to see Laura, one of my physical therapists. She asked if I had told my story. I said, "Three times last week." I no longer have needles in my feet, so I am walking one and a half miles each day.

While we were at the hospital, we saw Dr. Klava walking toward the elevator. "Dr. Klava, can I catch up with you?" I asked.

He turned and said, "I think you're going to."

We talked as we rode the elevator. "I don't wear the braces now. I use them only when I am out working with cattle."

He replied, "There's some sort of divine intervention in your recovery."

"I firmly believe that even if I don't deserve it."

"None of us do."

April. I can now stand on my toes for a while. The doctor said when I could stand on my toes, I would be up to 50 percent recovery. I told my story of faith to the Carrington Trinity Lutheran Confirmation group, a class of about forty to fifty teenagers. Some adults attended also. I spoke about half an hour. I read my tablet entries to them and then told about the hospital. Some looked at pictures. The kids broke up into groups to talk about it. It went well.

May. I stopped using air casts for chores. I thought I would see how it went lifting feed baskets for the cows. I went in the house and told Kaye, "Mark this day on the calendar. I will never have to wear braces again." That was one year and ten days after the accident.

I had another EMG test. Dr. Klava told me the nerve response was four times greater than it had been in the November 2004 test. He said, "You are in the bonus round now." He was very pleased with my progress.

During the spring and summer of 2005, I was able to do all my own fieldwork and calving out of the cows. There isn't a day that goes by that I don't stop and give thanks for God's grace and for my recovery.

January 2006. I shared my testimony with the men at the Cottonwood Assembly of God in Cottonwood, Arizona. Kaye shared hers with the women's group.

March. This last week, I have noticed that I have more natural feeling of walking.

May 3, 2006. Darrell Otto, my father-in-law, was admitted into Elim Care-Memory Care Unit in Fargo, two years to the day after my accident.

June 3, 2006. Twenty-five months after the accident, I climbed a forty-two-foot rock climbing wall in Woodbury, Minnesota.

# Closing

Before my accident, I had less of a commitment to God, and often I didn't recognize the need or have the desire to rely on Him for help. After the accident, things changed. I know God more and more. I have more of a commitment to Him as my Savior. I have more peace and thankfulness and the feeling of being truly blessed. It's a feeling of contentment, a desire for closeness, an understanding and satisfaction in being wanted and knowing eternity will be better than this life and the love of family, because of the promises in God's Word.

Before the accident, I knew God was there for me but stumbled to tell other people ... how to put my experiences into words. After my accident, it feels natural to give my testimony.

I have some additional thoughts about the accident. I never felt the need to ask the question, "Why did this happen to me?" I would not wish this to happen to my worst enemy, but for what I have gained, I would not trade it for anything. "He is no fool who gives what he cannot keep to gain what he cannot lose" (Jim Elliot, martyred twentieth-century missionary).

# Miracles

Some define miracles as a supernatural event by which God reveals Himself to humankind. I believe that God intervened in a series of miraculous ways during my accident and recovery to reveal Himself and call us to salvation and a closer relationship with Him.

There were several miracles involving the grain truck. As the truck was being pulled with a chain, the wheels lined up perfectly with the tractor wheels. As it caught up to the tractor, it climbed up the wheels and then came to a stop, landing on my legs (midthigh). As I lay flat on my stomach along the hood of the tractor, the bumper of the truck rested on my legs with just enough pressure to cause exquisite pain but not enough to break any bones or cause bleeding. Only God could keep the truck from causing death, bone fractures, and blood loss as it came down and rested on my legs.

As I lay there, God gave me the clarity of mind, the ability to reason, and the confidence to believe that Kaye could successfully drive the truck off my legs.

God kept me from going into shock so that I was awake and alert when Kaye got home and could instruct her in a clear, calm voice as to how to drive the truck off my legs.

The truck started when Kaye turned the key. It had been turned on for five hours as the truck rested on the tractor wheels at a forty-degree angle to the ground. For many days, I had been having trouble getting it to start, but miraculously, the engine started on the first turn of the key.

The pain that I experienced during those five hours was exquisite—very sharp and intense, caused by the passive stretching of the ischemic muscle of the compartment. It felt like putting one's finger in a vise grip, tightening it, and holding it there. I had a knife. I knew I could reach my heart. I just about ended my life. I submitted to God's will when I said, "Thy will be done." At that moment God intervened, flooding me with a sense of peace and assurance that overwhelms me to this day when I talk about it. I waited another two hours for Kaye to come home. It was because of God's grace, His goodness, that I chose life despite the pain.

I was not injured further as the bumper of the truck lifted up off my legs. Also, I don't know how I was able to hold on to the bars of the tractor as it moved off. As Kaye pushed down on the accelerator, the truck began to back off my legs, simultaneously sliding and lifting as it retreated and dropped to the ground.

Having Kaye drive the truck off my legs, instead of waiting for another way for it to be removed, saved my legs from amputation. I was in critical condition and had emergency surgery just in time for the compartmental pressure to be relieved and further damage stopped to muscle tissue and kidney function.

Only God could orchestrate the events for us to delay the start of surgeries to close my wounds, to choose another doctor, Dr. Abdullah, to close my wounds, and for Dr. Abdullah to agree to perform the series of surgeries. Dr. Abdullah's correct approach managed to repair more than seven feet of wounds that were subject to infection for about six weeks, resulting in no infection. His skill in the timing of the surgeries and his skill in attaching cadaver skin and suturing my wounds resulted in no rejection or skin grafts. The speed and success at which the cadaver skin adhered to the wound bed, creating vascular growth, allowed me to be in rehab within a week of the last surgery. Because no skin grafts were needed, I did not have to be transferred to the burn center in Minneapolis or risk developing an infection at the donor site. All progressed quickly with no setbacks. Glory to God!

All wounds were closed without using skin grafts from me. The defects of the lower third of the leg nearly always require free tissue transfer (skin grafts). Dr. Abdullah didn't think he could cover the last wound (1 x 4") without skin grafts. In the fourth surgery, he covered half of it with cadaver skin. A week later, he closed the wound completely and gave credit to God for the miracle of closing all wounds without using skin grafts.

My life was restored to wholeness in Christ Jesus. Only Jesus can do this work in one's heart. I was restored to physical, spiritual, and emotional wholeness because of the grace of God. I continue to live life to the fullest.

# Blessings

What are blessings? The word is used to express something good or beneficial that has been received. These are some of the blessings that George received from others and from scripture. Whatever challenges you may face, may you be encouraged by these. –Kaye

My pastors have had a great part in strengthening my faith, and I am deeply grateful for them, but I can honestly say I have grown most in faith by living with my wife. She has a very strong faith, and she has lived it. You might say I gained my faith through her faith. I couldn't ask for a better gift from God than the gift of Kaye (1 Cor 7:14 NIV).

Faith, Hope, and Love
And now these three remain: faith, hope and
love. But the greatest of these is love.
—1 Corinthians 13:13 NIV

Shortly after I was admitted to the hospital, our friends Les and Colleen gave me an inspirational calendar. I found so many words of hope and reassurance that God would be with me at all times from reading that and the Bible. There are thousands of promises in the Bible waiting to be claimed.

In my life, most of the moments of grace that have impacted me completely lose their power in the telling. Most people

write them off as coincidences. Yet I have found that it is through the little things that God communicates that He is very near. God is always with us. If our hearts are open to Him and hear his sometimes small voice, we will see that He reveals Himself to us every day of our lives.
—*Little Things* (devotional)

Karen, who flew from Arizona the day after the accident to be with me, conveyed the message from her pastor that he had prayed for a complete recovery, which were more words of assurance.

Jesus looked at them and said, "With man this is impossible, but with God all things are possible."
--Matthew 19:26 NIV

Dee and Darrell Otto, Kaye's parents, often brought food and treats to the hospital for family and friends. When our family was together during the first week, they brought meals, and they ate together in the family rooms. Tony Flach, nephew, brought soup and sandwiches, rolls and coffee. Family, friends, staff, pastors, and acquaintances gave us gifts of every kind. We were encouraged by their visits and their outpouring of love.

May the Lord make your love increase and overflow for each other and for everyone else, just as ours does for you.
--1 Thessalonians 3:12 NIV

Shirley Lyson, my sister, who was in contact with her sister-in-law, Gwendy, in Spokane, Washington, said that Gwendy even got some retired nuns to pray for me ... and I'm not even Catholic! Gwendy said, "At the nunnery where I work, each morning the sisters go to the prayer pool and get the list of all who need prayers. This is what they do the whole day. They pray constantly for those on the list, and your brother, George, will be prayed for by the sisters."

Later, when Shirley came to visit me, she said, "When those retired nuns pray, they get the job done." I was also on the prayer list of a group of nuns from England.

And pray in the Spirit on all occasions with all kinds
of prayers and requests. With this in mind, be alert
and always keep on praying for all the saints.
--Ephesians 6:18 NIV

"Peace Be Still"
(Original song written and composed by Karen Stewart.)
Based on Matthew 8:23–27

As the wind roared to life, as the waves came aboard,
They said, "You do not care, all of us will soon die."
But You said, "Peace be still," the sea obeyed your voice,
"Do you know it is I, the Great I Am."

All of us can relate, the storms come crashing in,
We say, "You do not care, why did you let this come."
But You say, "Peace be still, why don't you trust in Me,
Do you know it is I, the Great I Am."

So we say to the storm, you will not conquer us,
Our Lord is strong enough to keep us standing tall.
And You say, "Peace Be still, I am your victory,
Do you know it is I, the Great I Am."

"Why do you fear? Why do you fear? I
am He who calms the waves."
"Why do you fear? Why do you fear? I am He who loves you."
"Why do you fear? Why do you fear? I
am the one who died for you."

God is our refuge and strength, an ever-present help in trouble.
—Ps 46:1 NIV

"Cowboy Pride"
(Excerpt from *Cowboy Pride*, Kit Pharo, Pharo Cattle Company.)

I'm ashamed to admit that I have had to learn many things the hard way. It took many years for me to realize the importance of having a close and personal relationship with God. Having a relationship with God actually makes being a cowboy much easier and more enjoyable—and I don't think others view me as being less of a man because I believe and trust in God.

I can't begin to describe all the benefits of having a relationship with God. The more I trust and rely on God, the more he blesses me. I always have someone to turn to for guidance and reassurance. I don't have to fret and worry about things any more. God is my father, my partner, and my friend. The greatest benefit, though, to having a relationship with God is knowing where I will spend eternity.

In Matthew 18:3–4 NIV, Jesus says, *"Unless you change and become like little children, you will never enter the kingdom of heaven. Therefore, whoever humbles himself like this child is the greatest in the kingdom of heaven."*

Men, this is of utmost importance. God has called us to be the spiritual leaders of our households. This is a very serious responsibility that cannot be delegated to others. Please do not be afraid to drop your guard and get to know God. Don't let your pride get in the way.

"Attitude"
Charles Swindoll

The longer I live, the more I realize the impact of attitude on life. Attitude, to me, is more important than facts. It is more important than the past, than education, than money, than circumstances, than failures, than successes, than what other people think or say or do. It is more important than appearance, giftedness or skill. It will make or break a company ... a church ... a home. The remarkable thing is we have a choice every day regarding the attitude we will embrace for that day. We cannot change our past ... we cannot change the fact that people will act in a certain way. We cannot change the inevitable. The only thing we can do is play on the one string we have, and that is our attitude. I am convinced that life is 10% what happens to me and 90% how I react to it. And so it is with you ... we are in charge of our attitudes.

The inspirational authors remind us that when life hands us lemons, we should make lemonade. They don't have any words of advice for when the lemon truck completely runs us over. A child born out of wedlock: no baby is a mistake in God's eyes. A divorce or death: we are never ashamed or alone in the presence of God. A crisis we can't see an end to: a good time to drop to our knees in prayer.
—Author unknown

There Ain't No Loopholes …
(Kit Pharo, Pharo Cattle Company)
Q. Why was the lawyer skimming the Bible right before he died?
A. He was looking for loopholes!

There's no way out. Sooner or later, we are all going to die. While some will live a very long life, others will tragically die at a relatively young age. Death will come upon most of us with little, or no, advance notice.

I realize that death is a subject most people would rather not think about or discuss. If there was nothing after death, then it probably wouldn't be worth discussing. However, there is something after death. Our body will die, but our soul will go on living. That's great news, isn't it? Or is it?

God's word, the Bible, clearly says that there is a heaven and a hell. When we die we are destined to go to one or the other. There is no in-between and there are no other options. Do you know where you will spend eternity? That may be the most important question that you will ever be asked.

No matter how good we are or how hard we try to be good, we will never be able to earn or deserve a place in heaven. The only way we can get to heaven is by God's grace through our faith in his son, Jesus Christ. Have you accepted Jesus as your personal Lord and Savior? If not, when do you plan to do so? Please don't wait until it's too late.

In Hebrews 9:27–28 NIV we read, *"Just as man is destined to die once, and after that to face the judgment, so Christ was sacrificed once to take away the sins of many people; and he will appear a second time, not to bear sin, but to bring salvation to those who are waiting for him."*

While there are no loopholes to help us avoid death, the Bible does tell us how we can be assured of a place in heaven. Just knowing that we spend eternity in heaven makes it possible to actually look forward to death with absolutely no fear.

I encourage you to spend time reading your Bible. It is full of wisdom, promises and instruction. I also encourage you to find a Bible believing and teaching church to attend.

Nothing can ruin our lives because our earthly lives are not the end of the story. The only thing that could ruin eternity for us is to lose our faith, to give up on the one person who can save us from everything we fear. To turn away from God because of our own weakness is the worst, worst thing.
—Author unknown

[3] For what I received I passed on to you as of first importance[a]: that Christ died for our sins according to the Scriptures, [4] that he was buried, that he was raised on the third day according to the Scriptures, and that he appeared to Peter, and then to the Twelve."

1 Corinthians 15:3-5 (NIV)

It is God whom and with whom we travel, and while He is with us at the end of our journey, He is also at every stopping place.
—Elizabeth Elliot

Reflections "One Year Later-May 3, 2005" Andrea, Karen, Elizabeth (excerpts), Corey (full text.)

Dad,

It is truly inspiring how determined you have been to get back to normal. I have been thinking about the accident a lot lately. It makes me sad and grateful at the same time. Sad because of the pain you had to go through and grateful for your recovery. It is a miracle. Watching you grow in your faith has been inspiring, also. And I feel I have grown in my faith, too. Andrea

Westbow has permission to publish this. Andrea

Dad,

One thing in particular that stands out to me the most is God's faithfulness and love for us. Your faithfulness to God will bless our family for generations to come. Never quit giving your testimony, for it is by our testimony and the blood of the Lamb that we overcome. (Rev 12:11 NIV) With love, Karen and Tad

I give permission for Westbow to publish my thoughts. Karen Stewart

Dad, I prayed for you, and you were taken into surgery. God gave me a peace through all this that I cannot understand. A peace that no matter what, He was in control, and everything would work out for the best. Blessed assurance. I couldn't have asked for a better outcome. I am astonished by His work in your physical body…but even more in your spirit. We love you, Craig and Liz

I authorize you to publish these statements in the book. Liz

*God said, "My grace is sufficient for you, for my power is made perfect in weakness."*
2 *Corinthians* 12:9

*Dad & Mom,*

It is hard to imagine a year has gone by. In some respects it seems like it was just yesterday when we were all getting that phone call that no one ever wants to get. Yet, when I see the progress that you both have made physically, mentally, and spiritually, it seems like the accident was years ago.

As I have thought about and witnessed everything that has transpired since that first phone call, no single word can do justice to explain how our family has reacted, embraced, and loved each other through all of this. However, over the past year I have thought of several words that keep reminding me of various conversations, actions, and reactions that I hope that I never forget as those words are the POWER OF....

Passion- Dad's passion for Mom kept him from thinking irrationally and using his knife. During our first conversation in the hospital discussing the details of the accident (on Mother's Day no less), Dad told me that his love for Mom was the main reason he did not use his knife. If passion is defined by one's acts, this definitely meets the definition.

Optimism-Never a word of "Why me?" but an attitude of "What can I do with what I have?" Dad didn't focus on what went wrong during the accident, but what went right for him to be in the hospital rather than the alternative. From the initial doctor assessment of amputation, walking would require bi-lateral double prosthetics, to "throwing the wheelchair away" less than three months after the accident and walking with a cane, Dad's optimism was a driving force.

There have been various tragedies that have occurred throughout Grandpa's life (Ervin Topp) and Dad's and our aunt's lives, yet you wouldn't know it based on how everyone in the family chose to react to those situations. Now, maybe I'm only remembering the good things that I want to remember, but isn't that what optimism is about, focusing on the good and not the bad?

At Grandpa's funeral, I will never forget a comment that Royce made about Grandpa. He said that no matter what the weather was outside, he said Grandpa would say "Great weather we are having today!" Grandpa had this attitude even though Grandma Thelma had arthritis and was wheelchair bound for the last several years of her life until she passed away in 1967. I never really knew why Dad was so good in the kitchen and cooking, etc., until we were at the hospital, and Dad mentioned that he was the one that helped Grandpa with Grandma the most during those years.

Glenda has had arthritis for years and has endured many surgeries and pain-filled days. Yet whenever she would visit the farm, take me out to lunch during college, or invite me over for dinner, Glenda was always smiling, never giving an indication of the pain she was in. I don't know who told me this, but Glenda said that she has accepted the pain of arthritis in hopes that the rest of the family will never have to endure what she or Grandma had to endure.

Will- Dad never gave up. He didn't accept the current status, but he strived for a better result. While on the tractor, Dad willed himself to stay alert and not give in. Throughout the rehabilitation in the hospital and physical and occupational therapy, Dad willed himself to continue his physical progression.

Encouragement- Dad's feet have never stopped moving. Even going into surgery and the first week in ICU, Dad was moving his feet. Although it was not technically the movement that the doctors wanted to initially see to determine if Dad would be able to walk again, I will never forget the look on Dad's face the first time I was in the ICU room, and he moved his feet for me. Although Dad could not say anything because of the tube, I truly believe he wanted to say, "Don't worry about me. I am moving my feet." Dad was moving his feet not only to encourage himself but also to encourage the rest of us.

Reunion- I had never really realized this until we were sitting in the hospital one day. Why is it that sometimes through tragedy you learn more about your family in that brief period of time as compared to all the rest of the years that you know someone? The knowledge that I am referring to is deeper than brief conversations that families typically have during other get-togethers. It is discussions families have about feelings and reactions around events that everyone knew about but never discussed. These are the discussions that help console and comfort everyone as you realize that others have gone through similar tragedies in the past, and their stories help you cope with what you are going through.

Opportunity- Whether Dad and Mom realize it or not, this accident provided them with a great opportunity. All through the years, I can remember Dad and Mom were always willing to help neighbors when in need and always taught us to do what is right. The accident provided an opportunity for the community to return the past acts of neighborly kindness that Dad and Mom had shown to others.

Within five days, there were approximately thirty-five people on the farm to ensure the crops were planted, the fencing was repaired, the cattle were worked, and various other tasks were completed. I received a call from Jeff at 1:30 p.m. on Saturday, telling me that within the hour they were going to be done!! Another opportunity that was provided to Dad was the ability to "give up control."

Although I know there probably is still is a sense of urgency within Dad when it comes to completing the various tasks around the farm, I have not seen this since the first day he got the tube out in the ICU. I did not count the number of questions that he had regarding what the neighbor's plans were for the next day at the farm, but there were several as he was finally able to talk. However, after that first day, Dad was less concerned about the details and "gave up control." At a later point in the hospital, Dad told me that he realized that "we are all dispensable. We can control what we can, and we have to sometimes rely on others to make sure the work is taken care of."

Faith- Faith is what "saved" Dad that day on the tractor. I would listen to Dad tell his "story" in the hospital to relatives and friends about how he struggled with the pain and the situation he was in during the first 2 1/2 hours and then how a peacefulness came over his (although the pain was still there) when he asked the Lord to help him get through the situation he was in.

When he told a nurse who was caring for him about his story, she painted a picture of the Lord's right hand. Dad said, "It was the right hand of the Lord that came over me while on the tractor." As Dad's faith has blossomed, so has Mom's. Together, I see that they are closer than ever, and the passion for each other has grown even stronger.

The weekend that Dad got out of the hospital and came to the Twin Cities, I found out that he was going to write a book about the accident and how it transformed his faith. I cannot wait to read it once it's finished as it is hard for any one of us to walk the walk that Dad has taken during the past year. During the same conversation, I had mentioned that I was also thinking about writing a book as I don't want any of us to forget what we have learned about ourselves and our families. I also want to make sure our children and grandchildren understand that through tragedy comes strength.

For me, how we choose to react to tragedy is defined by the POWER OF....You possess each of those qualities, and I truly admire how you have demonstrated them throughout the past year. These are the qualities of a hero, and you are my hero. I only hope that I can demonstrate these same qualities to Ryan, Kyle, Justin, and Ethan so that they can pass them along to their children as well. I love you both, and I am so proud of how the both of you have changed during the past year.

I have one simple (maybe not so simple) request for the two of you and Andrea, Karen, and Liz. However, it does not need to be completed immediately. I would like each of you to write a paragraph or more on each of the above qualities to include in the book that I am going to write. As a family, we have become stronger through this tragedy. As a family, I would like us to tell our story to our future generations. I hope that you will look back on the day of May 3 and always think of the positive things that have occurred in your lives, as well as ours, as a result of this accident.

We love you very much. Corey, Rhonda, Ryan, Kyle, Justin, and Ethan

You most definitely have my permission for Westbow to publish it. Corey

Fiftieth Anniversary—August 18, 2018.

George and Kaye.

Rolling along for fifty years ... Topp Family 1968–2018.

Families

Dark Blue-Corey, Rhonda, Ryan, Ethan
Topp (Kyle, Justin missing)
Woodbury, MN

Light Blue-Andrea, Marlen, Paige, Garrett Haugen
Casselton, ND

Green-Karen, Tad, Cora, Calli, Cailyn Stewart
Sun Prairie, WI

Red-Elizabeth, Craig, Jaden, Gavin, Tegan Bjur
Fargo, ND

# Resources

CaringBridge: www.caringbridge.org/visitclassic. From the directory drop down box select "nd" and type "gtopp" in site name.

DVD testimony at Cottonwood Assembly, Cottonwood, AZ, January 30, 2006. Available by contacting George Topp at geotopp@daktel.com.

DVD testimony at Bethel Chapel, Carrington, ND, January 19, 2008. Available by contacting George Topp at geotopp@daktel.com.

"Peace Be Still" by Karen Stewart. Available by contacting Karen Stewart at tadandkaren@yahoo.com.

# Bibliography

Beauchamp, Evers, Mattox, W.B. Sauders. "Passive Stretching of the Ischemic Muscle." *Sabiston Textbook of Surgery: The Biological Basis of Modern Surgical Practice*, 16th ed. 2001.

"Ischemic Neuropathy Definitions," medical-dictionary. thefreedictionary.com.

"Miracles." https://ag.org/Beliefs/Topics-Index/Miracles.

Pharo Cattle Company. "Cowboy Pride" (November/December newsletter, 2002): 44017 County Road Z, Cheyenne Wells, Colorado 80810.

Pharo Cattle Company. "There Ain't No Loopholes" (January/February newsletter, 2005): 44017 County Road Z, Cheyenne Wells, Colorado 80810.

Stewart, Karen. "Peace Be Still."

# Appendix 1

## Kaye's Journal

As I approached the driveway and looked toward the farmyard, I saw the old International truck with its front end high in the air resting on the back end of the loader tractor. For a split second, I had no thoughts about what I had just seen. Then it registered in my mind: the truck had somehow reached the top of the tractor's back wheels and rested there looking as if the hood was gobbling up the tractor. I drove the car into the garage and parked. I was starting to feel anxious.

As I ran toward the back of the truck, I was scared. What would I find? I hoped that George would come from the nearby shop or from around the front of the truck and tell me what had just happened and that he hadn't gotten the truck down yet.

Rounding the back corner, I heard "Kaye" and saw George lying along the top of the tractor hood, his head turned away from me, both of his legs (mid-thigh) pinned under the bumper of the truck. What I had just seen told me that it was an impossible situation to get out of, and a thought flashed across my mind, "We aren't going to get out of this one this time and be OK. This is too bad." In that instant, in a split second my heart fell, and   simultaneously, a deep, dark sense of dread washed over me. How could he still be alive?

Then, George slowly lifted his head and turned to look in my direction, his face grimy, sweaty, and grimaced in pain.

He spoke, and hope arose. Slowly and deliberately, he said: "Get into the truck. See if it starts. I don't know if it will start, but if it does, you put it in reverse and you back it off and don't stop until it hits the ground."

"No! I'll go and get Dennis."

He repeated his words to me in the same manner, "No, you get into the truck. You start the truck and put it in reverse, and you don't stop until you hit the ground."

I ran around the front of the tractor to the truck door. It was open, but was up very high in the air. I didn't know if I could climb in, but I knew that I had to on the first try. I reached as high as I could and grabbed the handle bar on the door frame with my right hand and with my left hand, the arm rest below the door handle. With all my strength and will, I pulled myself up into the cab, grabbed the steering wheel with my left hand, and sat down on the seat.

As I positioned myself behind the wheel, pulling myself closer to it and stretching my left leg to reach the brake and clutch, I felt the staggering weight of doing this right. What would George's condition be after the truck was rolled off his legs? What would I see? Would he still be alive? I simply could not let my foot slip off the clutch or make a mistake and put it in the wrong gear.

I pushed in the clutch with my left foot and turned the key.

It started right up.

I looked for reverse on the floor shift, and before I covered it with my right hand, I looked again. The thought of shifting into a forward gear terrified me.

Then I moved the shift into reverse, pushed the gas pedal to the floor and held it there, gunning the engine. The truck moved back a little and lifted up. It seemed to stay suspended in the air for a split second, then rolled back down over the tractor wheels, and dropped to the ground with a loud bang and a final bounce. I turned off the key, jumped out of the truck, and started toward George.

All I could see was his back. His legs were hanging straight down. His feet were on the tractor's axle. He was holding onto the loader bar with his arms bent at the elbows. His head was resting on them.

I ran up to him. He asked for water. I rushed into the house and back out to George. He drank it down and then said, "Go get Dennis."

I ran as fast as I could to the garage, got into the car, and raced to Hofmanns'. I clutched the steering wheel with both hands and gasped continually for breath. The car skidded around the corner into their driveway, and I drove up onto the lawn, blowing the horn all the way and stopped at the front steps. I didn't see Dennis. I raced up the steps into the house. Evelyn was at the sink with her back to me and turned when I said, "George was in an accident. Where's Dennis?" She grabbed a towel to dry her hands and came toward me, saying, "He's in the yard." I ran outside, and Dennis was coming toward the house. Evelyn hollered that George had an accident. I took off with the car. Dennis followed with his old pick-up, and as I looked out the rear view mirror, I saw him a distance behind me. I parked behind the truck and ran to George. Dennis was right there.

I climbed onto the hood of the tractor, and as I placed myself to help lift George down, I glanced at the front of my new, yellow sweater and a fleeting thought crossed my mind, 'It's going to get covered in grease.' Dennis positioned George's feet, forecasting and explaining each move, and I grabbed around his shoulders.

We edged him down slowly. George stood upright like a post, and as Dennis steadied him, Dennis wrapped his arms around George's torso to hold him upright. Dennis hollered to Evelyn, who had parked behind the accident scene and couldn't see what was going on, to call 911 and get an air ambulance. She didn't know what had happened to George ... neither did Dennis. There was no time to talk.

I ran to get the car and drove up on the lawn, stopping between the house and the weeping birch in the back yard where the accident took place. The backseat was filled with shopping bags. As quickly as I could, I grabbed the bags and threw them out on the lawn. I had bought 4 glass bowls for a friend's wedding, and as I tossed them, I wondered if they would break. They didn't.

As Dennis was dragging George into the car, I got into the back behind the driver's seat, put my arms around George's shoulders and pulled. Dennis lifted his legs, telling him he would have to bend his knees to get his feet inside. He did not make a sound. Crouching behind the driver's seat, I held his head in my hands. It felt so small; his eyes so tiny.

Dennis got in. George desperately wanted and needed water. Dennis drove on the lawn, around the back of the house, and up onto the cement slab in front of the garage. He ran into the house, brought out a glass of water, and handed it to me.

George asked for water several times as we drove the 20 miles toward Carrington, the nearest town with a hospital. He lifted his head slightly to drink it. Some would run off the side of his face.

His face was sweaty and greasy, and he was drawing breath in and out through clenched teeth. He was shaking so. The pain was getting worse as we got closer to Carrington. Dennis drove fast, but he couldn't have driven fast enough for me. I talked to George all the way into town. Dennis would shout back, "George, you stay awake now. Are you awake?" Once I asked George if he wanted me to sing. He shook his head slightly and grimaced a little. I took that as a "no."

I tried to think of things to say, and when I would tell him to stay awake, he would nod his head "yes." I told him that God was in control and He would take care of Him and that I loved him and we would get through this together. I repeated those kinds of things many times.

George reached into his shirt pocket (it was difficult because he was shaking) and gave me a small green tablet. "Tried to make it until 2, then 3, then …"In and out of consciousness. Dropped the pencil at 3:30. Legs really hurt when truck backed off." (This was all George was able to tell me about the accident until five days later when he would no longer have a breathing tube.)

George spoke once again with an even weaker voice and with greater effort, "Tell Dennis to tell neighbor Leon: to finish seeding the barley, leave the truck with the drill fill running because the starter doesn't work, hook up the alternator for the bi-directional, and give the calves 8½ baskets of feed." I relayed each part of the message to Dennis. He would do as George asked.

Dennis drove into the emergency entrance of the hospital. Medics simultaneously opened both back doors. As they got George out of the backseat and onto a backboard, I told them that George had been pinned between a grain truck and a tractor. They moved him ever so carefully onto a cot. I followed them into the ER, and they started cutting off his clothes. I was shaking. Theresa Edland, lab tech, was standing nearby and had me sit down on a chair.

A few minutes later, I went out to the car, which was parked in the hospital lot, and using Evelyn's cell phone, called our oldest daughter Andrea and quickly went back into the ER to see George. He said his hips were starting to hurt.

Dennis, Evelyn, and I sat in the waiting room until the doctor came. He told us there was damage to George's thighs and possibly to his kidneys. There were no broken bones. He would be flown to Fargo by air ambulance. I asked if I could go with him. There wasn't room.

I rode home from Carrington with Evelyn. I called Andrea, who lived in Casselton, to give her an update and tell her my plans. Dennis and Evelyn would bring me to her place, and we would go into Fargo together. Casselton is only 20 miles west of Fargo. I called Karen in Cottonwood, Arizona, but was unsuccessful in reaching Corey in Woodbury, Minnesota, and Elizabeth in Fargo.

Evelyn helped me bring the packages from the backyard into the house, and Dennis fed the calves. I put more clothes into my suitcase which was already packed as I had stayed the night before with Bev, my sister, in Fargo. I took the phone book and my address book among other things. We stopped at Evelyn's so she could change her shirt and get deodorant. Then the three of us left for Andrea and Marlen's home near Casselton, a 1 ¾ hour trip.

As we traveled, I called and talked with Elizabeth and Rhonda, as well as neighbors and friends. Craig and Elizabeth headed for the hospital and saw the helicopter land on the roof of MeritCare's North Campus at 8:45 p.m. They were with George for 15 minutes before he was taken into surgery at 10:30 p.m. During that time, Glenda,

George's sister, talked with him on the phone. He was alert and oriented and able to move his legs.

Craig called and told me that George had said, "Five hours is a long time." Then Craig said, "George wants to talk to you." He handed the phone to George. There was a pause. When George spoke, he said one word, "Amputation." Craig took the phone from George and added, "If there is too much damage, Dr. Kubalak will amputate then."

When we arrived at Andrea's, we went into the house, greeted Andrea and Marlen, and I showed Dennis and Evelyn their antique staircase (a strange thing to want to do at that time-it was very beautiful, however). Andrea kissed Marlen goodbye, and she and I drove 20 miles to Meritcare on North Broadway in Fargo, arriving at 11:00 p.m.

Craig and Elizabeth met us at the emergency entrance and took us to the waiting room where my siblings, John and Bev and their spouses, Muriel and Dave, and nephew, Tony, were waiting. George had been in surgery for ½ hour.

Surgery lasted from 10:35 p.m. to 12:15 a.m.

Dr. Kubalak, surgeon, came into the waiting room to give us a report. They had cut open George's legs to relieve the pressure and to assess damage to the muscle tissue, making lateral cuts of both thighs and calf muscles. Dr. Kubalak said it would be 48 hours before he would know if the damage was reversible or irreversible. The other main concern was George's kidneys. Because his muscle tissue was compressed, the breakdown of this tissue could get into and damage kidney function. He told us the best case scenario was that George would be in ICU for one week, then on a regular floor, and rehab.

We had been quietly visiting before Dr. Kubalak came in. Bev had fallen asleep and slept through the doctor's report during which he had given us little hope George would keep his legs. Now, the mood was somber. No one talked. Muriel started praying the Lord's Prayer, and we all joined in. Then, I prayed.

As we left the hospital, Bev and Dave invited me to stay with them at their home in north Fargo for the duration of George's stay in the hospital. I accepted.

# Appendix 2

## Kaye's Journal

May 4, Tuesday morning. 5:45 a.m. Numb. I woke up this morning with these words and tune playing in my head, "This is the day of new beginnings, time to remember and move on, time to believe what love is bringing, laying to rest the pain that's gone. Christ is alive, and goes before us to show and share what love can do. This is a day of new beginnings; our God is making all things new." I slid out of bed, onto my knees, to pray. Bev and I went to Darrell and Dee Otto's, our parents, to tell them about the accident but didn't talk about the possibility of amputation. We stayed there until the folks had time to absorb the news and seemed OK. Then we went to the hospital to see George.

George was sedated and didn't keep his eyes open very long. He was on a ventilator and couldn't speak. Roger Topp, cousin, and Dale and Diane Rosenberg, friends, were standing in the hall when I came out of the hospital's family room. Roger was near the door, leaning against the wall and crying, "What happened?"

I didn't know.

# Appendix 3

## Kaye's Journal

May 5, Wednesday morning-I am so anxious that I slept only 4–5 hours. The kids and I are to make the decision as to whether George will keep or lose his legs.

Before going through the ICU doors to see his dad, Corey motioned to me to come alongside him, hugged me, and cried and cried. At 2:00 p.m. the doctor reported to the five of us in the hall. We discussed what he said before going back into the waiting room to tell others. There, we all prayed. Alan Scanson called to say, "Everything at the farm is OK. Nothing to worry about. Flat out done."

# Appendix 4

## Kaye's Journal

May 6, Thursday morning. Weepy. I appreciate and am so thankful to be staying with Bev and Dave. Their love and friendship is precious to me, and their help invaluable. Their home is a sanctuary. I need the quiet and relaxing surroundings. The hospital is so busy.

# Appendix 5

## Kaye's Journal

May 7, Friday morning. Praying, thanking, praising, and thinking of the impact of this. I am living in the moment: getting exercise, eating well, sleeping good, having a place of repose at the end of the day yet waking up very early in the morning. Then I'm off to the hospital where there is activity all the time: doctors, calls, visits, emails, decisions about farm work, getting things in order, social worker, insurance; so much, so fast, but all with the help and comfort from so many family and friends. We have been thrust into the hearts and minds of many. We are ready and willing to follow God's lead as has been revealed to us by His Spirit.

Funny … I am using one of Bev's cars, but when I left the house for the hospital this morning, I couldn't get it into reverse! Bev had to get out of her car, run across the street, and help me!

# Appendix 6

## Kaye's Journal

May 8, Saturday morning. I am praying for a complete recovery. I talked with Corey about speaking with the plastic surgeon and asking him about the wisdom of starting skin grafts on Monday. George was moved out of ICU at 1:00 p.m. and to the sixth floor, surgical unit. Jeff Topp, cousin and friend, called Corey. Crop seeding at our place was done at 2:00 p.m.

# Appendix 7

## Kaye's Journal

May 9, Sunday, Mother's Day. Up at 6:00 a.m. I walked for twenty minutes, thinking about what we will learn from George about the accident. I want Corey and the girls to spend time alone with their Dad and talk: tender times, precious moments.

George & I read scripture and a passage from the Upper Room, devotional, and talked about how George could stand the excruciating pain. "I just about gave up. At 3:30, I knew I could make it. I didn't want to be a coward, and I kept going because of my love for you, Kaye. I would fade in and out, but I believe I was awake 90% of the time."

Corey visited with his dad and then all of us met at Elizabeth's. We sat in a circle in the living room. Corey began by telling us that George was in so much pain that he almost ended his life. "He had a knife. He knew he could reach his heart. Dad didn't want to be a coward or do that to his family, and he didn't want mom to find him, what it would look like." I gasped and layed my head on Corey's shoulder and cried. Then, I said, "Your dad's legacy to us will be one of love and extraordinary strength."

Karen added, "If you're in that much pain, you're going to try to get out of it. God will turn every situation into good for His glory. Especially if there are thousands praying. God sees the end from the beginning and gets us there."

We went out to eat for lunch. I had a hard time eating or enjoying anything because I kept thinking about George and the pain he endured. It made me sick to think of it. My only consolation was that George knew it was good for him to talk about it. The kids gave me a card with messages from each of them, a massage, mums, and a green plant.

# Appendix 8

## Kaye's Journal

May 10, Monday morning. I woke up thinking about how George is doing emotionally because of what Corey told us yesterday. I talked again with Bev and Dave about skin grafting and headed for the hospital. George, "I listened as Kaye read Psalm 107. That is just what I felt at 3:30 on the day of the accident, that God was with me every step of the way. God wouldn't give me any more pain than I can bear. I knew that at 3:30. God has things for me to do." Andrea had an ultrasound this morning to find out if she was having a boy or a girl. After telling Marlen, she told us the exciting news, "It's a boy!"

# Appendix 9

## Kaye's Journal

May 11, Tuesday morning- I was thinking about the emotional and spiritual healing that is taking place because George is able to talk about the five hours and when he hit a low point. Because of the surgery being delayed, God has given us more days to work through this. Karen and I are here alone with George. We are treasuring this time with him.

I read Isaiah 12 and "The Power of Prayer" (Upper Room). Karen laid her hands across her dad's legs as she prayed for healing.

George asked if I had the notebook. I did. He told us that after he had dropped the pencil, he had held so tightly to the notebook. He was affected by emotion, making it difficult to talk. Then he described one scene in the movie, "The Passion," which he, Elizabeth, and Craig saw on Good Friday. It was unusual for him to have gone to a movie that day because it was the beginning of a holiday weekend and we had kids home, but Elizabeth really wanted to go, so he went. He said he didn't cry once during the movie, but he was emotional as he talked about the flashback scene in which Mary, the mother of Jesus, was crying as she looked into Jesus' face when he fell in front of her while carrying the cross. Mary saw Jesus as a child and reached out to pick him up.

Then added George, "I didn't cry during the entire five hours. (Pain will take everything, even your tears).

George was very worried about me and asked how I was doing, if I was getting enough sleep. Corey expressed concern for me, too. I told George that I have had such love and support from our kids, family, and friends that I was doing OK. But I was really touched by his concern.

# Appendix 10

## Kaye's Journal

June 19. As we were driving on the gravel road to the east of the farm, we saw Jeff Edland spraying in the soybean field to the north. Leon was waiting in the truck which was parked nearby. We stopped along the road. George opened the door of the car and still sitting in the back seat on the passenger's side put his legs outside onto the gravel. Looking to the north he watched as Jeff stopped the sprayer and got off. Both men walked to the car. Jeff reached down and George firmly clasped his hand and held on to it, swinging his arm back and forth before letting go. Jeff stepped aside. George held out his hand to Leon and he took it. Leon leaned in and grabbed George around the neck with his left arm and buried his head in his shoulder and they cried. They held their embrace for several minutes and then George said, "Friends forever."

# Appendix 11

## Kaye's Journal

June 20. After church, we drove to the barley field up north and stopped to visit with Deloris Wright. Alan Scanson, Lester and Jill Wright, Patti and Ray, and Dennis and Evelyn came to the house to see us. Toward evening, we drove back to the hospital for the last week of rehab.

# Appendix 12

## Kyle Topp Interview

On May 24, 2014, Kyle Topp, grandson, Woodbury High School sophomore, Woodbury, MN wrote the following:

> I was wondering if you would answer these questions in the next couple of days for me for my English class. You can either go with the first answer(s) that comes to your head or spend your time on it, but either way will be just as good. Thanks! Kyle
>
> Q. How do you deal with challenges in life?
> A. By having an optimistic attitude and faith about my life. Also, if plan A doesn't work, I am ready to go to plan B.
>
> Q. What is a life experience that has shaped who you are?
> A. Ten years ago on May 3, 2004, I was pinned for five hours on a tractor with a truck on top of me. The bumper of the truck was on top of my legs, and my legs were on a bar of the loader on the tractor.

Q. How did you deal with this challenge?

A. While being pinned and in great pain, I was writing my good-byes, and I found out that I was completely helpless. I had been looking at my watch every five minutes for two hours. At the end of the two hours, I dropped my pencil. It was a very low point for me. Although I was in extreme pain, I said to myself, "My legs aren't broken, and I'm not bleeding to death." I got very bold with God, and I said, "God, you are not through with me yet. I will make it. Come what may, I will wait for Kaye to come." Grandma was at a meeting in Fargo. My cell "bag" phone was in the truck. I then said, "Thy will be done," and the most complete peace came over me. I didn't look at my watch until 5:00 p.m. Kaye came at 6:00 p.m.

Q. Did this difficulty bring out the best or worst in you?

A. I believe it brought out the best in me by building on my faith in God.

Q. Why do you believe there are challenges in life?

A. Challenges are there to build character. We are either beaten down or we are built up. We can have the attitude that this is the first day of the rest of my life, or we can dwell on, "Oh, what has happened to me?" This doesn't do any good.

Q. What are your strengths?

A. Helping others.

Q. What are your weaknesses?

A. My temper.

Q. What are you most proud of?
A. My twelve wonderful grandkids, my four grown and successful children and spouses, and my lovely wife. She is where I got my faith.

Q. What do you like to do?
A. Fish, hunt, garden, and work with cattle. Oh, did I tell you that I like to fish? Ha, ha.

Q. What is your biggest regret?
A. Being short with my wife.

Q. What is your biggest fear?
A. Not living up to my grandkids' expectations or my grandkids not reaching something that they are capable of. Never be afraid of failure. I will be proud of them no matter what the outcome.

Q. Who are your heroes?
A. God

Q. What's your favorite childhood memory?
A. Scoring twenty points in a basketball game.

Q. What qualities do you believe are good to have and why? What qualities are bad and why?
A. Being a friend to people and keeping a good attitude in life. Not willing to learn from your mistakes.

# Appendix 13

## Photos of Open Wounds

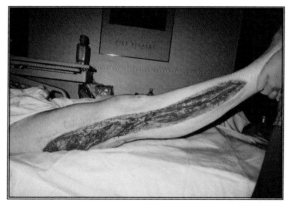

Right leg—exterior.

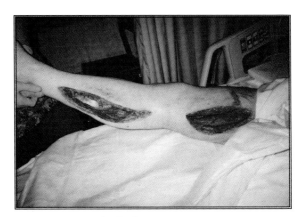

Right leg—interior.

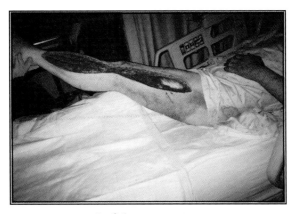

Left leg—exterior.

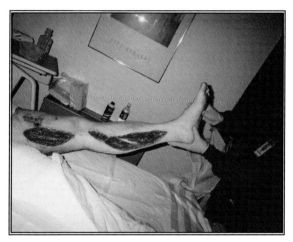

Left leg—interior.

# Glossary

**bilateral**: Relating both to the right and left side of the body or of a body structure.

**compartment syndrome**: The compression of nerves and blood vessels within an enclosed space, leading to impaired blood flow and nerve damage. Passive stretching of the ischemic muscle of the compartment in question causes exquisite pain, pain out of proportion to the injury. It must be emphasized that over time this pain will diminish as further ischemia occurs.

**distal**: situated away from the center of the body or from the point of origin; specifically applied to the extremity or distant part of a limb or organ.

**fasciotomy**: Procedure to relieve tension or pressure and loss of circulation if compartment syndrome threatens muscle death or nerve damage.

**hypesthesia**: diminished sensitivity to stimulation.

**ischemia**: Ischemia is an insufficient supply of blood to an organ, usually due to a blocked artery.

**ischemic:** A low oxygen state usually due to obstruction of the arterial blood supply or inadequate blood flow, leading to hypoxia in the tissue.

**ischemic neuropathy:** Neuropathy resulting from acute or chronic ischemia of the involved nerves.

**neuropathy:** A general term denoting functional disturbances and/or pathological changes in the peripheral nervous system.

**peripheral nervous system:** The entire complex of nerves that leave the confines of the brain and the spinal cord (the central nervous system) to supply the muscles, skeleton, organs, and glands.

**renal failure:** Kidney failure.

**rhabdomyolysis:** Rapid destruction of skeletal muscle, resulting in leakage into the urine of the muscle protein myoglobin.

# About the Authors

**George**

I grew up on a farm at Grace City in east central North Dakota. At the age of seventy-four, my wife, Kaye, and I are still living on the farmstead where I was raised.

At age three, my mother, Thelma, started getting rheumatoid arthritis. Her age was thirty-eight, and my three sisters who were eight, six, and five years older than me did the household chores to help Mom out. She was confined to a wheelchair when I was in grade school. We had some very good friends, Phyllane Wold and Sophie Topp, who would help out on wash day or cleaning the house. My cousin, Dorothy Hareland, would come during the summers to work for us while I was a teenager. Her birthday was ten days before mine, so she would always say she was older and wiser than me and I had to listen to her.

When Glenda, the youngest of my three sisters, graduated from high school and went off to college, the duty of washing, bandaging, dressing, and helping Mom get to and from bed was put on me. My dad didn't make me do it, and I never thought it was odd to be the one to help her. When you have a job to do, you just do it. That attitude has stuck with me all my life and gave me compassion for others less fortunate than me.

All during my youth, I helped Dad, Ervin, with farm work. I had a great love of farming and working with cattle. Dad was a 4-H leader for twenty-five years, and I loved showing cattle at the county fair in Carrington. I was in 4-H for ten years and was a leader for thirty years.

I graduated from high school in 1963, and in August 1967, Mom passed away at age fifty-seven. In the spring of that year, my second cousin, Marvin Topp, age seventeen, died in a tractor PTO (power take-off shaft) accident. Mom made the comment, "I wish it was me." It was a blessing to see her pass, because I know she is in a better place.

By then, I was farming full-time with my dad and took over the farm. Dad was always there to help. We had a good working relationship. He passed away in 1985 when he was seventy-nine years old.

In 1968, I was lucky enough to marry a gem, Kaye Otto. She has a very strong Christian faith. Happy to say it rubbed off on me. We are blessed with one son, three daughters, one special daughter-in-law, three special sons-in-law, seven grandsons, and five granddaughters, ages six to twenty-three.

To our grandchildren, I would say it is such a blessing to watch you grow up. Each and every one of you is so special to Kaye and me. You have so many strong qualities, and the potential is endless for you. Set your sights high. You are capable of so much. Remember—if you stumble and fall, at least you are going forward. Don't look back. Live for today because yesterday is past, tomorrow has yet to come, and today is the present—a gift from God.

There are several things that have proved to be true in my life. One is this: attitude is everything, so pick a good one. The other is this: when you find out you have nothing left but God, that's when you find out He is all you need.

It is our prayer that you, as well as each reader, will be encouraged by my story. My experience is proof that God is great, and with Him, anything is possible. Jesus is my rescuer. He wants to be yours too.

## Kaye

Ah, now I, Kaye, can write. I have so much on my heart to share. It's been bottled up for a long time waiting for this opportunity to put my thoughts in writing. George's story of the accident is my story also. I was alongside him every step of the way. I could not bear his pain or be a substitute for his recovery, but I was there.

I know God prepared me for his accident. I know because I experienced it. For a very long time—months, even years—I had been struggling with being too busy, not having the time to do what needed to get done or having time to do the things I wanted to do.

So in this state of unease and at the suggestion of a good friend and coteacher, Glenda Hoeckle, I began reading Benny Hinn's, *Good Morning, Holy Spirit*. Glenda lent me her book in February or March 2004. As I read the book, my life was greatly impacted. I'd wake up in the morning and say, "Good morning, Holy Spirit." For the very first time, I could feel the presence of the Holy Spirit engulfing me and going before me as I began each new day. I had felt the love of God and His presence for a long time in my life but never in the way I did since reading the book. There is a tangible sense of Him engulfing, guiding, and protecting me.

It was at this time that I began to think about wanting time to read and study, and to be doing more things with George and helping him. Could I cut back from teaching and teach three days a week instead of four? I prayed about it. George and I talked about it. I asked my superintendent if this would be possible. He agreed to three days.

It was a difficult thing to know I would be making less money (it wasn't for George), but school would continue to pay the full amount I had been receiving in health insurance. We made the decision rather quickly and without much hassle. Then I told friends I had resigned. My letter of resignation was accepted by the school board, and I was issued a new contract to teach three days a week (Monday through Wednesday) at the elementary school, Binford only. Cutting back a day wouldn't hurt the Title 1 program in the elementary too much. I would no longer be teaching in the junior-senior high at Glenfield, however. So my work week, thirty miles away from the farm, was all set for the fall of 2004, and this schedule made it possible for me to leave George for the day while he was recovering from the accident.

After making the decision, my attitude about getting things done changed. I could allow myself to do other things because I had two days every week in addition to the weekend, which had been rush-rush. In addition to the feelings of frustration of not getting caught up on the weekend were the thoughts of the work involved with starting a new workweek schedule.

I also saw God's hand in preparing George. For some reason, I was determined that he would see the movie *The Passion*. Would that happen? I didn't know. I didn't want to see it on the big screen but would have done so with George (closing my eyes for much of it). After much indecision, he went with Elizabeth and Craig on Good Friday. I stayed home and waited for Corey's family to come for Easter weekend.

The next morning, I asked George about the movie. It was hard for him to talk about it, as he was so emotional. The most difficult scene was when Mary had a flashback of Jesus as a small boy. He was falling, and she reached to pick him up. Jesus was in front of her with the cross. The other flashbacks were hard for George too.

On the night of May 3, as Andrea and I drove to the hospital, I was thinking of all of this and my life experiences in general and said, "God has been preparing me for such a time as this. We have been thrust into the lives of so many." From the time that I found George on the tractor and until long after he was well again, I was proactive in helping him emotionally and spiritually. I could do little for his physical needs but could initiate times when God would guide and comfort both of us. We prayed, read, sang, and talked. I, as well as others, knew the importance of his talking about the events of the accident—details of what he remembered, what he saw, what he felt—and the importance of us listening without solving or minimizing his revelations. Layer after layer began to be exposed. We held each other as we cried, and we laughed too, although there wasn't anything to laugh about when we talked about the accident itself. And then came the first time when George stood up from his wheelchair and hugged me. It was so amazing for us to feel each other's bodies in this way again, and he was thrilled to be standing on his own two feet.

The intimate times with each other and God sustained us and gave us hope. In addition, journaling every day helped me to debrief and keep details clear. Staying at the end of each day in Bev and Dave's home gave them the opportunity to support and help us when we needed it the most. They had our backs.

George made it easier for all of us with his sense of humor and his determination to be okay as he could be. I never once in all that time heard him complain. His attitude was positive even through the most challenging circumstances. However, one of the things that I would have done differently would have been to limit calls and visitors so he could get more rest. Because George freely welcomed people either in person or on the phone and talking was beneficial for him, I didn't realize his need for more rest. But surgeries, morphine, and his rehab schedule took their toll, and his physical and emotional endurance was at a max by the time he began to recover at home. Mine too.

I, like George, wouldn't wish an accident like this on anyone, but I, unlike George, would trade it. It was so hard, but in all that, we knew God was in every moment, and He provided all that we needed, at the time that we needed it. Our story is evidence of His sovereignty, His power, His love, His grace, His mercy, and His healing. He was more than enough, and we were heartened time and time again, and for all that, we are undeserving but ever so grateful and thankful. Glory!

1 Peter 1:6-9 (NIV)

[6] In all this you greatly rejoice, though now for a little while you may have had to suffer grief in all kinds of trials. [7] These have come so that the proven genuineness of your faith—of greater worth than gold, which perishes even though refined by fire—may result in praise, glory and honor when Jesus Christ is revealed. [8] Though you have not seen him, you love him; and even though you do not see him now, you believe in him and are filled with an inexpressible and glorious joy, [9] for you are receiving the end result of your faith, the salvation of your souls.